I0797368

20 MINUTE AIR FRYER

CHRISTINA KYNIGOS

DK [RED]

20 MINUTE AIR FRYER

EASY HIGH-PROTEIN MEALS UNDER 600 CALORIES

CONTENTS

Welcome

I am so excited to welcome you to my fourth cookbook ... wow. What a feeling. How did I even get here?

If you don't know me, hey, I'm Christina! A Greek-Cypriot who LOVES food. I've never trained as a professional chef but I learned all about cooking from my grandparents whom I lived with growing up. Their passion for food and the delicious meals they put on the table inspired me from a very early age, and I've been developing my skills ever since, learning more and more every day.

I've been sharing my personal brand of low-calorie, high-protein meals online since 2020. For me, food is here to be enjoyed. My recipes are low in calories but full of flavour – so whatever your motivation, whether it's losing weight or keeping an eye on your macros, you can be sure you'll feel fully satisfied.

Cooking is a huge part of my life – but since having my daughter, I've found that I am often short on time and energy (it turns out toddlers are hard work). So, I started looking for ways to create delicious meals that I can get on the table quickly and easily – and that meant making use of everyone's favourite kitchen gadget, the air fryer. Now I've decided to gather those ideas together in the book you're holding, so you can enjoy them too! All the recipes have four things in common:

- They are easy to follow – I mean *really* easy.
- They take 20 minutes or less to make.
- They contain fewer than 600 calories per serving (more on this on page 13).
- They are delicious.

I'm super excited for you to try these recipes and to love your air fryer as much as I do. Tag me on social media so I can see your amazing creations – and let's get cooking!

Christina x

About this book

I've divided the book into five chapters, each one packed with flavour and exciting ideas, covering everything from speedy lunches to special occasions.

NO-STRESS LUNCH

This chapter is all about grabbing something quick and easy to keep you going through the day, whether you're working from home, need to take something with you to the office, or are just looking for a speedy way to keep everyone happy. My **Tuscan Chicken Salad Jars** (page 26) are the perfect prep-ahead lunch, while the **Honey-Sriracha Salmon Poke Bowl** (page 45) is a delicious light bite that will keep you satisfied all afternoon. I've also shared a few of my favourite brunch-style recipes, so there really is something for everyone.

FAMILY FAVOURITES

If you're used to cooking for a family, you'll know it can be tricky finding meals that everyone will enjoy while still keeping things both healthy and delicious. This chapter is packed with all my secret weapons for when you're standing in front of the fridge after a long day and need to get something on the table fast. My **Sticky Paprika Halloumi Gyros** (page 66) are always a hit, while the **Mini Kyiv Bites with Creamy Mash** on page 74 are sure to become a regular request from your family.

MEAL-PREPPED & READY TO GO

One of the best ways to take the stress out of cooking is to prep ahead. Rather than turning to supermarket ready meals, this chapter is all about recipes that can be prepared in advance and then reheated or finished on the day. I like to spend a bit of time on a Sunday doing meal prep so that I'm ready to tackle the week ahead with a fridge full of my favourites. Highlights here include my **Creamy Cheesy Sausage Gnocchi** (page 97) and **Hot Honey Beef & Sweet Potato Bowls** (page 106).

BETTER THAN TAKEOUT

Trust me, I know how tempting it can be to reach for the phone and order out when you're tired and hungry. But food deliveries often take an age to arrive, and when they do come they can be disappointing. From the outrageously good **Inside-Out BBQ Bacon Cheeseburger** (page 126) to my very own **Tandoori Butter Chicken** (page 134), the recipes in this chapter are my very best "fakeaways": homemade versions of all your favourite takeout foods, with a few playful twists – and a fraction of the calories. They're easy to make and completely delicious – and they'll be ready before the pizza delivery driver has even started their engine.

DATE-NIGHT BANGERS

Nothing says "I love you" like a homecooked meal. Whether you're trying to treat your partner or a new love interest, or want to whip up something special for a dear friend or someone in your family, the recipes in this chapter are sure to impress. From the **Peri Peri Steak & Garlic Butter Frites** (page 154) to the **Triple-Cheese Lasagne** (page 157), they taste indulgent and look amazing – just don't let your loved one know how easy they are to make!

Why air-fry?

Air fryers are currently taking over the food world – and it's easy to see why. They save you both time and money, as they cook foods more quickly and efficiently than a conventional oven, meaning your energy bills will be significantly lower. They also deliver the same delicious results as conventional cooking methods, but you don't need to use anywhere near as much oil, meaning they're often a healthier way to cook.

In case you hadn't guessed, I'm a little bit obsessed with my air fryer – but if you don't have one, I've got you covered. I've included alternative cooking methods for every recipe, so you can still cook from this book using a conventional oven or stove top. This might mean it takes a bit longer to cook, but the food will still be mouth-wateringly good.

AIR FRYER HINTS, TIPS & HACKS

Types of air fryer

I'm a big fan of a two-drawer air fryer, as it allows you to cook two things at once, which is great if you're meal-prepping or have a family to feed. If it's just you, you might want to opt for a smaller model, as a one-drawer air fryer uses a lot less space. Some air fryers are super fancy and have loads of different settings and functions, but to keep things simple, I've made sure all the recipes in this book can be made using the basic 'air fryer' setting, whatever model you have.

Timings and temperature

I tested the recipes in this book using my Ninja Foodi Dual Zone Air Fryer. As with conventional ovens, the temperatures of different air fryers may vary slightly, which means cooking times will vary slightly too. Use the timings in this book as a guide and always check the food while it's cooking. Investing in a digital probe thermometer is a good idea, as this allows you to check the internal temperature of the food you're cooking – a great way to confirm that meat is fully cooked.

Preheating your air fryer

I haven't included preheating instructions for each recipe, but I normally preheat my air fryer to 200°C (390°F) for 4–5 minutes before adjusting the temperature as needed and adding the food. You may need to experiment a little with your own air fryer to find the approach that works best for your make and model, but this is a good starting guideline.

Crisper plate

The crisper plate is the removeable plate that comes with most air fryers. When you place the food you're cooking directly on the crisper plate, the hot air circulates all around it, helping it to crisp up nicely. In this book, if I don't mention *removing* the crisper plate, then assume I'm putting the food directly on to it. And here's a tip – for anything that's coated in breadcrumbs, I normally spray the crisper plate with oil first to stop the food from sticking.

For recipes that involve a sauce, like lasagne or mac and cheese, you can either use an ovenproof dish that fits into your air fryer (though these can be tricky to remove), or you can remove the crisper plate and just add your ingredients directly to the air fryer basket. Silicone liners can come in handy when you're doing this, but they aren't essential.

How the recipes work

My focus for this book has been to find quick and easy ways to make foods you actually want to eat. As far as I'm concerned, carbs are life, sauces and drizzles are delightful, and everyone deserves texture, flavour, and fun – so why restrict yourself? My philosophy is that everything can be enjoyed in moderation. It's all about balance: enjoying healthy food without compromising on flavour.

A NOTE ON CALORIES

As I mentioned earlier, using an air fryer is typically a healthier way of cooking as less oil is required, and so for this book I've made a few tweaks to ensure that each of these meals comes in at under 600 calories per serving. This can be handy if you're watching your calories, helping you to remain in-line with the recommended daily intake, while still leaving room for a snack and a drink.

Depending on your health goals, you might find macro-tracking useful, so with that in mind I have provided nutritional information for each recipe. This includes the calories, as well as macros like protein, fat, and carbs. I've made every recipe in the book high in protein so you will feel full and satisfied after every meal.

The macros and calories in ingredients will vary from brand to brand, so if you are tracking closely I suggest adding the ingredients you buy into a calorie-calculator app to get the most accurate information. Any extra serving suggestions shown as a "Tip" or marked as "optional" in the recipes have not been included in the calorie and macro calculations, so you'll need to bear this in mind too.

A NOTE ON SYMBOLS

For every recipe, I've included some at-a-glance info to help you see how long it will take to prepare (things like chopping, peeling, and so on), how long it will take to cook (this time refers to the air-fryer method; the conventional method may take slightly longer), and how many people it serves. I've also included a symbol to highlight those recipes that are suitable for freezing.

▲ **Prep** 5 mins

● **Cook** 8 mins

■ **Serves** 1

✱ **Freeze**

A NOTE ON INGREDIENTS

Throughout the book, I've chosen the best ingredients for each dish to ensure that every recipe meets my 20-minute time limit. This means that some recipes use pouches of pre-cooked microwaveable rice, while others use dry basmati rice that is cooked as part of the recipe. Similarly, some recipes call for shop-bought fries, while others use homemade fries. Typically, I've used shop-bought fries when the recipe only calls for a small quantity, or when I needed to keep things speedy, but if you'd rather make your own, you can use the recipe on page 109 as a guideline (though the quantities may need adjusting accordingly).

Likewise, in order to meet the required calories and macros, I have often used low-fat or fat-free yogurt, cheese, cream, etc. You are welcome to use your preferred versions of these ingredients, but just bear in mind that these changes will affect the macros.

SHOP IT

Below are some of the ingredient types I used while testing these recipes – and which I use regularly in my own kitchen. It's completely up to you whether you adopt the same approach – though again, if you are tracking macros and calories, you may want to use a tracking app so you can add the precise ingredients you choose.

SPRAY OIL	You can find bottles of spray cooking oil in the supermarket, but I like to buy a spray bottle online and fill it with olive oil – it works just the same.
LOW-FAT BUTTER	I use low-fat butter as it's less calorific than full-fat, and also has less saturated fat – win-win! All low-fat butters will have a range of different calorie content, but I use one that has around 45 calories per 10g serving.
HOT SAUCE	Everyone has their own favourite brand of hot sauce, and it's the perfect ingredient to amp up the flavour! My favourite is Frank's RedHot Original, which is easy to come by in the supermarket.
FAT-FREE GREEK YOGURT	My Cypriot roots mean that I love authentic Greek yogurt. There are lots of great fat-free Greek yogurts to choose from – I'd look out for ones that are less than 100 calories per 100g serving.
SHOP-BOUGHT SKIN-ON FRIES	I love carbs! In this book you'll see lots of recipes that include a handful of fries. When making small amounts of fries, it's much more convenient to use shop-bought skin-on fries, rather than making homemade. There are plenty of supermarket varieties to choose from that come frozen and aren't too expensive.
CREAM	Cooking with cream can be tricky, as creams with a lower fat content can easily split when heated. I like to use an alternative to cream, such as Elmlea, which means I can keep an eye on calorie intake while also using something that's less likely to split.
CHEESE	A 50 per cent lighter Cheddar cheese is a great way to satisfy your cheesy cravings while also being mindful of calories. There are also high-protein, low-fat brands available that taste amazing!
TORTILLA WRAPS	Tortilla wraps feature in many of my recipes – they're an absolute staple for me. Most people use them for tacos and burritos, or even as a sandwich alternative at lunchtime. I do that, too but I also love to maximize their versatility and mix it up with pizza-inspired wraps, taco "pancakes", smash burger-style wraps ... The possibilities are endless!

WHEN ALL YOU WANT IS AN EASY LIFE AND SOMETHING QUICK YET DELICIOUS FOR LUNCH, I'VE GOT YOU COVERED. THESE RECIPES REQUIRE MINIMAL PREP BUT DELIVER ON FLAVOUR, WITH EVERYTHING FROM SALADS AND WRAPS TO TOASTIES AND EVEN TACOS!

NO-STRESS LUNCH

Hot honey halloumi pasta salad

Prep 5 mins
Cook 10 mins
Serves 2

This pasta salad is the perfect balance of sweet, salty, and savoury, with crispy halloumi, a drizzle of spicy honey, and hearty pasta. It's a light yet satisfying dish ideal for lunch or even as a side at your next gathering.

120g (4¼oz) dry fusilli (or any pasta shape)
spray oil
150g (5½oz) low-fat halloumi, cubed
1 tbsp honey
½ tsp chilli flakes
handful of rocket (arugula)
¼ cucumber, diced
2 tomatoes, deseeded and diced
30g (1oz) sun-dried tomatoes, drained and sliced

For the dressing
2 tsp honey
squeeze of lemon juice
pinch of chilli flakes

Cook the pasta according to the packet instructions, then drain and set aside to cool.

Remove the crisper tray from the air fryer. Spray the halloumi with oil and air-fry at 200°C (390°F) for 4–5 minutes or until nicely browned, then drizzle with the honey and sprinkle over the chilli flakes. Air-fry for a further 1–2 minutes until sticky.

Alternatively, spray a frying pan with oil and fry the halloumi over a high heat for 5–6 minutes, making sure it has browned nicely all over. Drizzle with the honey and add the chilli flakes. Mix well and cook for 2–3 minutes more, making sure all the halloumi is coated in the hot honey.

Combine the drained pasta, rocket, cucumber, and fresh and sun-dried tomatoes in a large bowl, then add the cooked halloumi.

Combine the dressing ingredients in a pan over a high heat and warm through for 30 seconds, then drizzle over the salad and serve.

TIP Any leftovers will keep in an airtight container in the refrigerator for 3-4 days.

KCAL	CARBS	PROTEIN	FAT
486	59G	27G	16G

Honey-pepper chicken bite snack wraps

Prep 5 mins
Cook 12 mins
Serves 2

These are inspired by a popular fast-food product – but my version is a lot healthier. Chicken bites are coated in panko and covered in sauce for a prep-ahead lunch option – or serve with fries for a delicious dinner.

250g (9oz) chicken breast, diced
1 tsp paprika
1 egg, whisked
30g (1oz) breadcrumbs
4 mini tortilla wraps
2 tbsp light mayonnaise
2 handfuls of iceberg lettuce, sliced
50g (1¾oz) cucumber, sliced
30g (1oz) grated mozzarella
salt and freshly ground black pepper

For the sauce
2 tsp honey
1 tsp freshly ground black pepper
2 tsp soy sauce
1 tsp hot sauce
1 tsp minced garlic

In a bowl, mix together the sauce ingredients, then set aside.

Season the diced chicken with the paprika, and salt and pepper to taste. Dip the chicken pieces into the whisked egg and then the breadcrumbs, turning to coat. Air-fry at 190°C (375°F) for 12 minutes or until cooked through. Alternatively, cook in an oven preheated to 200°C (180°C fan/400°F/Gas 6) for 15–20 minutes, turning halfway.

Tip the crispy chicken bites into the bowl of sauce and turn to coat, then return them to the air fryer or oven for an extra 1–2 minutes until sticky.

Spread each wrap with mayonnaise, then top with sliced lettuce, cucumber, mozzarella, and sticky chicken. Wrap and enjoy!

TIP Try this with tofu for a veggie version.

KCAL	CARBS	PROTEIN	FAT
490	52G	45G	11G

Prep-ahead pizza muffins

Prep 5 mins
Cook 15 mins
Serves 4
Freeze

These pizza muffins are a game-changer for busy days. Packed with all your favourite pizza flavours, they're delicious, easy to make, and perfectly portable, making them ideal for quick lunches, snacks, or dinner on the go.

- 2 eggs, plus 200g (7oz) egg whites (from about 7 eggs)
- pinch of chilli flakes
- 8 cherry tomatoes, diced
- handful of spinach, chopped
- 4 pepperoni slices, quartered
- 400g (14oz) chicken mince (ground chicken) or chicken sausages
- 1½ tsp dried oregano
- 1 heaped tbsp tomato purée
- 4 English muffins, halved
- 4 low-fat cheese singles
- salt and freshly ground black pepper

Find an ovenproof dish that fits in your air fryer and line with baking parchment.

In a large bowl, whisk together the eggs and egg whites, then season with a generous amount of salt and pepper, along with a good pinch of chilli flakes. Stir in the cherry tomatoes and spinach, and top with the pepperoni. Transfer to the prepared dish and air-fry at 190°C (375°F) for 10–12 minutes or until cooked through. Alternatively, cook in an oven preheated to 200°C (180°C fan/400°F/Gas 6) for 20 minutes.

Meanwhile, season the chicken mince with a good pinch of salt and pepper, then mix in the oregano and tomato purée. Wet your hands and roll the mixture into 8 equal-sized balls, then shape these into patties. Spray a frying pan with oil and cook the patties over a medium heat for a few minutes on each side until cooked through, working in batches if necessary.

Once the omelette is ready, divide into quarters. If you're eating right away, lightly toast the muffins (skip this step if you're prepping ahead), then place a slice of omelette inside each one, along with 2 chicken patties. Top with the cheese slices. Enjoy your filled muffins straight away, or wrap in foil and store in the fridge for 3–4 days (see tip).

KCAL	CARBS	PROTEIN	FAT
418	33G	39G	14G

TIP To reheat the muffins, unwrap and heat in the microwave at 600W for 30 seconds, then flip and heat for a further 30-40 seconds. Alternatively, air-fry (still wrapped in foil) at 180°C (350°F) for 10 minutes until warmed through.

Fluffy pancakes with bacon & maple syrup

Prep 5 mins
Cook 8 mins
Serves 1
Freeze

Perfect for breakfast, brunch, or even lunch, these pancakes offer a delicious combo of sweet and savoury. With crispy bacon and a generous pour of maple syrup, they're light, fluffy, and totally indulgent.

100g (3½oz) full-fat cottage cheese
1 egg
30g (1oz) self-raising flour (or plain/all-purpose flour with ½ tsp baking powder and ⅛ tsp salt)
pinch of ground cinnamon
1 tsp powdered or granulated sweetener (or use sugar)
spray oil
2 smoked bacon medallions
1 heaped tsp maple syrup
handful of blueberries

You will need 2 round 10cm (4in) silicone cooking moulds

TIP You can blend the mixture before cooking to get rid of any cottage cheese lumps for a smoother pancake.

In a large bowl, combine the cottage cheese, egg, flour, cinnamon, and sweetener, and mix until combined (see tip).

If using the air fryer, spray your silicone moulds with oil and divide the mixture equally between them. Air-fry at 160°C (320°F) for 8 minutes, then turn them over and remove the moulds. Air-fry on the other side at 180°C (350°F) for a further 3 minutes or until cooked through.

Alternatively, spray a frying pan with oil and fry ladlefuls of the batter over a low–medium heat for around 4 minutes on each side, or until cooked. This method won't get the pancakes quite as fluffy, but they'll still taste banging!

Air-fry the bacon at 200°C (390°F) for 4 minutes until crisp. Alternatively, grill (broil) on high for 6–8 minutes. Slice.

Serve the pancakes topped with the bacon, finished with a drizzle of maple syrup and the blueberries.

KCAL	CARBS	PROTEIN	FAT
362	32G	30G	13G

Tuscan chicken salad jars

Prep 5 mins
Cook 14 mins
Serves 2
Freeze (chicken only)

Bright and flavourful Tuscan flavours, including sun-dried tomatoes and basil, mixed with chicken and an addictive dressing. A perfect prep-ahead lunch for busy days.

2 × 150g (5½oz) chicken breasts
1 tsp Italian seasoning
spray oil
10 cherry tomatoes, diced
40g (1¼oz) sun-dried tomatoes, drained and diced
handful of spinach, finely sliced
1 small red onion, finely diced
4–5 basil leaves, sliced
salt and freshly ground black pepper

For the dressing
100g (3½oz) fat-free Greek yogurt
50g (1¾oz) low-fat mayonnaise
1 tsp oil from the sun-dried tomato jar
1 tsp Italian seasoning
1 tsp garlic granules
pinch of chilli flakes

In a bowl or jar, combine all the dressing ingredients with 2 tablespoons water. Season with salt and pepper, mix well and set aside in the fridge.

Season the chicken breasts with salt and pepper, and sprinkle with the Italian seasoning. Spray with oil and air-fry at 190°C (375°F) for 7 minutes, then flip and cook for another 7 minutes until cooked through. Alternatively, cook in an oven preheated to 220°C (200°C fan/425°F/Gas 7) for 18–20 minutes until cooked through.

Dice the cooked chicken and add to a large bowl. Add the remaining salad ingredients and mix well.

Grab two large lidded jars. Divide the dressing between the two jars, then top with the salad. Cover and store in the fridge for 3–4 days.

Once you're ready to eat, tip out the contents of the jar, making sure all the dressing comes out too, and give it a good mix!

KCAL	CARBS	PROTEIN	FAT
302	12G	44G	8G

Tuna & avocado toastie

Inspired by a favourite sandwich from a café I love, but with my own twist. Who'd have thought pesto would go so well with tuna? I mix this up regularly and use a toasted bagel or pitta if I fancy a change.

160g (5¾oz) canned tuna in spring water, drained
3–4 jarred jalapeños, diced
3 tbsp low-fat mayonnaise
1 tbsp fat-free Greek yogurt
2 tsp shop-bought low-fat green pesto
2 slices low-calorie bread
spray oil
2 tomato slices
25g (scant 1oz) avocado, sliced
a few dashes of hot sauce or Tabasco (optional)
salt and freshly ground black pepper

In a bowl, mix the tuna with the jalapeños, mayonnaise, and Greek yogurt, then season with salt and pepper.

Spread the pesto over the bread slices, then top with the tuna and close to make a sandwich, gently pressing down. Spray the sandwich with oil and air-fry at 200°C (390°F) for 2–3 minutes until browned. Carefully turn it over, spray again and air-fry for a further 2 minutes. Alternatively, spray a frying pan with oil and fry the sandwich over a medium heat for 3 minutes on each side.

Carefully open the toastie and add the tomato slices and avocado, along with a little hot sauce or Tabasco, if you like. Close it up once more and enjoy.

KCAL	CARBS	PROTEIN	FAT
393	32G	40G	11G

Pepperoni flatbread pizza

I love traditional Detroit-style pizza, which has a thick, airy crust with a signature square shape. For this version, to keep the calories low, I've opted for an easy shop-bought flatbread, while keeping all those delicious flavours.

1 flatbread (about 80g/2¾oz)
1 tbsp tomato purée
pinch of dried oregano
40g (1¼oz) low-fat cheese, grated
4 pepperoni slices
3–4 jalapeño slices, chopped

Spread the tomato purée over the flatbread, then sprinkle over the oregano. Top with the grated cheese, pepperoni slices, and jalapeños.

Air-fry at 190°C (375°F) for 6–8 minutes until the cheese is melted and golden. Alternatively, cook in an oven preheated to 180°C (160°C fan/350°F/Gas 4) for 10–15 minutes.

Serve and enjoy.

KCAL	CARBS	PROTEIN	FAT
386	35G	28G	14G

Spicy chicken & ranch wraps

Prep 5 mins
Cook 9–10 mins
Serves 2

I'm not sure about you, but hot sauce is my absolute favourite sauce on this planet, so I had to add a few recipes that used this holy concoction. Here, I teamed it up with the creaminess of ranch to balance out the flavours.

250g (9oz) chicken breast, butterflied
1 tsp cayenne pepper
spray oil
1 tbsp hot sauce (I use Frank's), plus extra to serve
40g (1¼oz) low-fat cream cheese
2 tortilla wraps
30g (1oz) low-fat Cheddar, grated
10g (¼oz) tortilla chips, lightly crushed (I like to use ones with a spicy flavour)
40g (1¼oz) iceberg lettuce, sliced
salt and freshly ground black pepper

For the ranch dressing
45g (1½oz) Greek yogurt
2 tbsp low-fat mayonnaise
1 tsp white rice vinegar
1 garlic clove, minced
½ tsp onion granules
½ tsp dried parsley
½ tsp dried dill

In a small bowl, combine the ranch dressing ingredients with 1 tablespoon cold water. Mix well and season with salt and pepper, then set aside.

Season the chicken with salt, pepper, and the cayenne pepper. Spray with oil and air-fry at 200°C (390°F) for 8–12 minutes, or until cooked through. Alternatively, spray a frying pan with oil and fry the chicken over a medium heat for 4–5 minutes on each side.

Shred the cooked chicken using two forks, then add the chicken to a bowl with the hot sauce and cream cheese, stirring to coat.

Make a single cut from the centre of each tortilla to the edge. Imagine each tortilla has been divided into quarters. Add the cheese to one quarter, the shredded chicken and crushed tortilla chips to the next, the lettuce to the third, and the ranch dressing to the last. Fold the tortillas, starting at the cut, so that the quarters sit on top of each other, forming a triangle.

Spray with oil and air-fry at 200°C (390°F) for 3 minutes until golden, or spray a frying pan with oil and cook for 2–3 minutes on each side. I like to add a dash of hot sauce before devouring!

KCAL	CARBS	PROTEIN	FAT
437	37G	45G	11G

Chorizo brunch potatoes

Prep 5-10 mins
Cook 20 mins
Serves 2
Freeze

This recipe is all about bold flavours and banging textures: crispy roasted potatoes, paired with spicy chorizo pieces and topped with fresh herbs.

400g (14oz) potatoes, cut into 2cm (¾in) cubes
2 tsp Cajun seasoning
50g (1¾oz) chorizo, diced
1 small onion, finely diced
½ red (bell) pepper, finely diced
1 tsp dried parsley
20g (¾oz) tomato purée
1 tbsp tomato ketchup
3 eggs, plus 3 egg whites
30g (1oz) low-fat Cheddar, grated
fresh chives, to taste
salt and freshly ground black pepper

Season the potato chunks with a good pinch of salt and pepper, along with 1 teaspoon of the Cajun seasoning. Air-fry at 200°C (390°F) for 15–20 minutes, shaking every 5 minutes until crispy and browned. Alternatively, cook in an oven preheated to 200°C (180°C fan/400°F/Gas 6) for 25–35 minutes, stirring halfway through.

Fry the chorizo in a frying pan over a high heat for a few minutes to release the oils, then add the onion and red pepper. Fry for a further 3 minutes, then season with salt and pepper. Add the remaining 1 teaspoon Cajun seasoning, along with the dried parsley, tomato purée, tomato ketchup, and a dash of boiling water. Mix well and cook for a minute more, then stir in the crispy potatoes.

Spray a separate pan with oil, then add the eggs and egg whites and cook over a low heat, stirring to scramble. Once the eggs are cooked to your liking, season with salt and pepper, then add the grated cheese and fresh chives to taste. Serve the eggs over or alongside the chorizo-tossed crispy potatoes.

KCAL	CARBS	PROTEIN	FAT
440	44G	30G	16G

All-day breakfast burrito

Prep 5 mins
Cook 10 mins
Serves 1
Freeze

I could eat burritos for breakfast, lunch, or dinner. This recipe can be customized to whatever your heart desires (or whatever you have in the fridge).

1 low-fat sausage
spray oil
30g (1oz) onion, finely diced
½ red (bell) pepper, finely diced
2 eggs plus 2 egg whites, whisked
1 tortilla wrap
25g (scant 1oz) low-fat Cheddar, grated
salt and freshly ground black pepper

Air-fry the sausage at 190°C (375°F) for 10 minutes or until cooked through. Alternatively, fry in a frying pan over a low–medium heat for 15 minutes, turning occasionally. Once cooked, slice the sausage.

Meanwhile, spray a frying pan with oil and fry the onion and pepper over a medium heat for a few minutes to soften. Move the veggies to one side of the pan, then add the eggs to the other, stirring to scramble. Once the eggs are cooked to your liking, season with salt and pepper and mix with the veggies.

Scrape the contents of the pan into the middle of the tortilla wrap, then top with the grated cheese and sliced sausage. Roll up the wrap and spray it with oil, then air-fry at 200°C (390°F) for 3 minutes until browned. Alternatively, spray a frying pan with oil and fry over a medium heat for a few minutes.

Serve and enjoy.

TIP I like to serve this with a dash of hot sauce, sriracha, or tomato ketchup!

KCAL	CARBS	PROTEIN	FAT
458	32G	37G	19G

Chilli jam panko prawns

Prep 5-10 mins
Cook 10 mins
Serves 2
Freeze

Prawns coated in crunchy panko breadcrumbs and drizzled with tangy chilli jam? Yes please. I could inhale these just by themselves, but the sticky rice is the perfect pairing.

- 4 tbsp low-fat mayonnaise
- 2 tbsp shop-bought sweet chilli jam
- 250g (9oz) raw prawns (shrimp), deshelled and deveined
- ½ tsp garlic granules
- 1 tsp paprika
- 35g (generous 1oz) panko breadcrumbs
- 250g (9oz) pouch microwaveable sticky rice (or use precooked rice)
- 1 spring onion (green onion), sliced
- pinch of black sesame seeds
- salt

In a small bowl, combine the mayonnaise, sweet chilli jam, and 1 tablespoon water. Mix well, then scoop half the mixture into a separate bowl. Set the first bowl aside, and add the prawns to the second. Stir to coat. Tip the breadcrumbs, garlic granules, and paprika into a third bowl and stir, then add the prawns, tossing to coat.

Spray the coated prawns with oil and air-fry at 200°C (390°F) for 8–10 minutes. For best results, use a crisper tray and ensure the prawns are well spread out, working in batches if needed. Alternatively, arrange the coated prawns on a lined baking tray, spray with oil and cook in an oven preheated to 180°C (160°C fan/350°F/Gas 4) for 10–15 minutes.

Meanwhile, prepare the rice according to the packet instructions.

Once the prawns are cooked, season with a pinch of salt, then serve with the sticky rice. Top with the sliced spring onions, drizzle over the remaining sauce, and scatter over the sesame seeds to finish.

TIP If you like a kick, add a drizzle of sriracha at the end!

KCAL	CARBS	PROTEIN	FAT
443	70G	30G	5G

Banging club sandwich

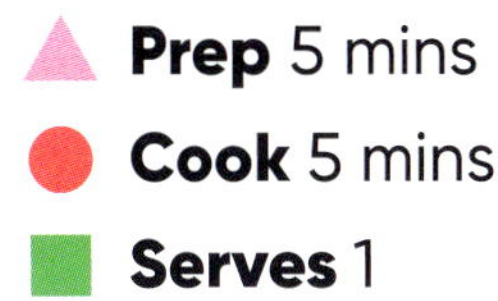

I absolutely love club sandwiches. They fill me up for hours, keeping me super-satisfied. If you're really hungry, this sandwich tastes amazing with some skin-on fries on the side!

100g (3½oz) chicken breast
spray oil
2 smoked bacon medallions
1 egg
3 slices of low-calorie bread (I used Warburtons Lighter Danish)
2 tbsp low-fat mayonnaise
handful of lettuce, sliced
1 tomato, sliced
salt and freshly ground black pepper

Season the chicken with salt and pepper, then spray with oil. Air-fry at 190°C (375°F) for 9–10 minutes, adding the bacon medallions 4 minutes before the end of the cooking time. Alternatively, spray a frying pan with oil and fry the chicken over a low–medium heat for 4–5 minutes on each side or until cooked through, adding the bacon medallions for the final few minutes. Let the chicken rest before slicing.

Meanwhile, spray a frying pan with oil and fry the egg to your liking.

Toast the bread, then spread 2 of the slices with the mayonnaise. Top one with half the lettuce, tomato, chicken, and bacon, followed by the other slice of toast with mayonnaise. Add the rest of the lettuce, tomato, chicken, and bacon, then top with the fried egg. Season with salt and pepper, then add the last piece of toast on top.

Slice, then dive right in!

TIP For extra flavour, season the chicken with 1 tsp Knorr Aromat Seasoning before cooking.

KCAL	CARBS	PROTEIN	FAT
426	43G	40G	10G

Thai-style peanut crunch salad

Prep 5 mins
Cook 8-10 mins
Serves 2

I am a big believer that a salad can be made banging, not boring. This Thai-style salad has so many amazing flavours, while the peanuts add a satisfying crunch. It's sure to earn a regular spot on your meal-plan rotation.

1 tsp soy sauce
1 tsp honey
2 × 150g (5½oz) chicken breasts, butterflied
40g (1¼oz) green cabbage, shredded
½ red (bell) pepper, finely diced
1 carrot, shredded
1 spring onion (green onion), sliced
1 coriander (cilantro) sprig, finely diced
10g (¼oz) dry-roasted peanuts, roughly crushed

For the sauce
1 heaped tbsp peanut butter (crunchy or smooth!)
1 garlic clove, minced
2.5cm (1in) piece of fresh root ginger, minced
1 tsp soy sauce
1 tsp sesame oil
1 tsp rice wine vinegar
1 tbsp sriracha
1 tsp granulated sugar or sweetener

In a bowl, whisk together all the sauce ingredients, along with 2 tablespoons cold water to loosen. Set aside.

Drizzle the soy sauce and honey over the chicken, then air-fry at 200°C (390°F) for 8–10 minutes or until cooked. Alternatively, spray a frying pan with oil and fry the chicken over a low–medium heat for 4–5 minutes on each side.

Leave the cooked chicken to rest for 2 minutes, then shred using two forks. Add to a large bowl, along with the cabbage, red pepper, carrot, spring onion, and coriander.

Mix well, then add the sauce and stir to coat. Finish with the crushed peanuts.

TIP This salad doesn't go soggy, so it's great to prep ahead. It will keep in an airtight container in the refrigerator for 3-4 days.

KCAL	CARBS	PROTEIN	FAT
337	16G	41G	12G

Honey-sriracha salmon poke bowl

Prep 5 mins
Cook 8 mins
Serves 2
Freeze (rice, salmon + edamame)

Salmon is one of my favourite types of fish. I adore the flavour, especially when it's enhanced with a kick of sriracha and a sweet dash of honey to balance it out perfectly.

2 × 125g (4½oz) skinless salmon fillets, sliced into chunks
spray oil (optional)
225g (8oz) microwaveable sticky rice (or use precooked rice)
60g (2oz) podded edamame beans
50g (1¾oz) cucumber, diced
1 spring onion (green onion), sliced

For the sriracha mayo
3 tbsp light mayonnaise
1 heaped tsp sriracha

For the marinade
2 garlic cloves, minced
2 tsp soy sauce
2 tsp sriracha
1 tsp honey
pinch of chilli flakes

In a bowl, mix together the sriracha mayo ingredients with 1 tablespoon water. Set aside.

In a separate bowl, combine the marinade ingredients. Add the salmon and stir to coat, then air-fry at 190°C (375°F) for 7–8 minutes. Alternatively, spray a frying pan with oil and fry the salmon over a medium heat for 6–7 minutes until cooked.

Meanwhile, prepare the rice according to the packet instructions.

Serve the salmon with the sticky rice, edamame, cucumber, and spring onion, drizzled with the sriracha mayo.

TIP For extra flavour and nutrients, add some diced avocado to your plate.

KCAL	CARBS	PROTEIN	FAT
595	53G	33G	28G

Taco crunch wrap

Prep 5 mins
Cook 5 mins
Serves 2

This is one of my most popular recipes – and for very good reason. It's crammed full of so many amazing ingredients, and every mouthful is a bite from heaven.

- spray oil
- 200g (7oz) lean beef mince (ground beef)
- 1 heaped tbsp taco seasoning
- 70g (2¼oz) shop-bought salsa
- 1 beef stock cube
- 2 large tortilla wraps
- 40g (1¼oz) low-fat Cheddar, grated
- handful of iceberg lettuce, shredded
- 5 cherry tomatoes, finely diced
- 20g (¾oz) red onion, finely diced
- 2 tbsp sour cream
- a few tortilla chips
- 2 mini tortilla wraps

Spray a frying pan with oil, then fry the beef mince over a medium heat for a few minutes to brown. Add the taco seasoning, along with half the salsa, then crumble over the stock cube. Add a dash of boiling water, if needed, to loosen. Stir well to combine, then allow to cool slightly.

Lay out the 2 large tortilla wraps and divide the beef mince between them, placing it in the middle. Top with the cheese, lettuce, tomatoes, onion, sour cream, and tortilla chips. Place a mini tortilla wrap on top of each one, then tightly fold the edges of the large tortilla wraps towards the centre, creating pleats.

Carefully place these bundles in the air fryer, folded-side down. Spray with oil and air-fry at 200°C (390°F) for a few minutes before flipping and cooking on the other side for a few minutes more until browned. For best results, use the crisper plate. Depending on the size of your air fryer, you may need to cook these one at a time. Alternatively, spray a frying pan with oil and fry over a medium heat for a few minutes on each side.

Serve and enjoy.

KCAL	CARBS	PROTEIN	FAT
543	57G	38G	17G

Crispy tofu satay noodles

Prep 5 mins
Cook 10 mins
Serves 2
Freeze (tofu + noodles)

When we eat vegetarian dishes at home, I include tofu almost every time. It's super versatile and soaks up any flavour you add to it. I like to serve it crispy, as I just adore the texture it brings to any dish.

200g (7oz) firm tofu
2 tsp soy sauce
1½ tsp curry powder
25g (scant 1 oz) cornflour (cornstarch)
spray oil
100g (3½oz) rice noodles
100g (3½oz) red cabbage, thinly sliced
100g (3½oz) mangetout (snow peas) thinly sliced
1 large carrot, thinly sliced
1 spring onion (green onion), sliced

For the satay
20g (¾oz) smooth peanut butter
1 tsp honey
1 tsp soy sauce
squeeze of lime juice

Combine the satay ingredients in a small jar with 1 tablespoon water and give it a good shake. If needed, add extra water to loosen. Set aside.

Using your hands, tear the tofu into small chunks. Season with the soy sauce and curry powder, then toss in the cornflour to coat.

Spray the tofu with oil and air-fry at 190°C (375°F) for 10 minutes until crispy, shaking halfway through and spraying with more oil. Alternatively, cook in an oven preheated to 200°C (180°C fan/400°F/Gas 6) for 20–25 minutes.

Meanwhile, cook the rice noodles according to the packet instructions, then drain.

Serve the tofu with the noodles and sliced veggies. Drizzle the satay sauce over the top and enjoy.

KCAL	CARBS	PROTEIN	FAT
595	70G	33G	20G

Chicken & bacon Caesar smash tacos

Prep 5 mins
Cook 12 mins
Serves 2

Craving a fresh twist on tacos? These little treats combine the creamy goodness of Caesar salad with crispy chicken, all wrapped in tasty tortilla. Perfect for mixing up your usual taco routine!

100g (3½oz) shop-bought skin-on fries
2 smoked streaky bacon rashers (slices)
300g (10oz) chicken mince (ground chicken) or chicken sausages
4 mini tortilla wraps
1 tsp mixed herbs or Italian seasoning
spray oil
2 handfuls of romaine lettuce, sliced
4 tbsp shop-bought light Caesar dressing
salt and freshly ground black pepper

Cook the fries according to the packet instructions.

Air-fry the bacon at 200°C (390°F) for 4 minutes until crisp. Alternatively, grill (broil) on high for 6–8 minutes. Slice and set aside.

Roll the chicken mince or sausage meat into 4 equal-sized balls, then press down each ball into the centre of a mini tortilla wrap (if using chicken sausages, I find it easier using a spatula to spread the chicken meat!). Season with the mixed herbs or Italian seasoning, then spray with oil and air-fry at 200°C (390°F) for 4–5 minutes, or until the chicken is cooked. If you have a two-drawer air fryer, use both drawers, or cook in batches to avoid overcrowding.

Alternatively, spray a large pan with oil and place over a medium heat. Fry the mini tortillas, chicken-side down, for 4 minutes or until cooked through. Spray the top of each mini tortilla with more oil, then carefully flip and fry for a further 2 minutes until the tortillas have browned. Again, you may need to work in batches.

To serve, pile the lettuce on top of the tacos, along with the fries and bacon, and drizzle with the Caesar dressing.

KCAL	CARBS	PROTEIN	FAT
502	54G	38G	14G

EASY, SIMPLE DINNER IDEAS THE WHOLE FAMILY WILL LOVE. NO FUSS, FULL OF FLAVOUR AND CERTAIN TO BE ON YOUR MENU WEEK AFTER WEEK.

FAMILY FAVOURITES

Sticky hunter's chicken tacos

Prep 5 mins
Cook 15 mins
Serves 2
Freeze (filling only)

Hunter's chicken but in taco form, with a drizzle of sticky honey and crispy bacon pieces to finish. It's heaven on a plate.

2 smoked streaky bacon rashers (slices)
300g (10oz) chicken breast, butterflied
2½ tsp barbecue seasoning
spray oil
1 small red onion, finely diced
½ red (bell) pepper, finely diced
140g (5oz) passata
1 chicken stock cube
3 tbsp barbecue sauce
4 mini tortilla wraps
50g (1¾oz) grated mozzarella
1½ tsp honey
salt and freshly ground black pepper

Air-fry the bacon at 200°C (390°F) for 4 minutes until crisp. Alternatively, grill (broil) for 6–8 minutes under a hot grill.

Season the chicken with salt and pepper, then sprinkle with the barbecue seasoning. Spray a frying pan with oil and fry over a high heat for 4 minutes on each side or until cooked. Remove the chicken from the pan, then dice and set aside.

Spray the same frying pan with more oil, then return to the heat and fry the onion and pepper for a few minutes until softened. Return the chicken to the pan, along with the passata and barbecue sauce. Crumble in the stock cube and add a dash of boiling water. Fry for 1 minute more.

Dip each tortilla wrap into the pan so that the sauce coats one side. Divide the chicken mixture evenly between the wraps, then top with the cheese and fold, with the sauce-dipped sides on the outside. Spray the tacos with oil and air-fry at 200°C (390°F) for 3 minutes until crispy. If I've got time, I like to flip the tacos, spray them again and cook for the same amount of time on the other side. Alternatively, spray a frying pan with oil and fry the tacos over a medium heat for around 3 minutes on each side, working in batches.

To finish, heat the honey in the microwave for 10–15 seconds, then brush it over the tortillas. Dice the cooked bacon and scatter it over the top, making sure it sticks to the honey. Serve and enjoy!

KCAL	CARBS	PROTEIN	FAT
545	53G	53G	13G

Chorizo, bacon & sausage orzo

Prep 5 mins
Cook 20 mins
Serves 4
Freeze

Crispy chorizo, sausage, and bacon pieces mixed with orzo and single cream combine to make an easy but delish dish full of all the meaty flavours.

200g (7oz) orzo
50g ($1\frac{3}{4}$oz) chorizo, diced
4 bacon rashers (slices), diced
1 onion, finely diced
8 reduced-fat pork sausages, skin removed and meat broken into chunks
3 garlic cloves, minced
100ml ($3\frac{1}{2}$fl oz) single (half and half) cream or alternative
1 chicken stock cube
30g (1oz) Parmesan, grated
flat-leaf parsley, to taste
freshly ground black pepper

Cook the orzo according to the packet instructions, then drain, reserving 1 ladleful of the pasta water. (If you are using the stovetop method, skip this step.)

Air-fry the chorizo and bacon at 200°C (390°F) without the crisper plate for 4 minutes, then remove and set aside. Add the onion and sausage meat, then stir to coat in the oil released by the chorizo. Air-fry for 6 minutes, then stir in the garlic and air-fry for a further 5–6 minutes, or until the meat is cooked through. Stir in the orzo and cream, then crumble in the stock cube. Add the reserved pasta water and air-fry for 1–2 minutes more.

Alternatively, fry the chorizo in a frying pan over a low–medium heat, then remove and set aside. Add the onion and bacon to the pan and fry for a few minutes until the onion softens and the bacon gets crispy. Add the garlic and sausage meat, then increase the heat to medium and fry for 3–4 minutes to give the meat some colour.

Dissolve the stock cube in 480ml (2 cups/$15\frac{1}{2}$fl oz) boiling water, then pour into the pan. Add the dry orzo and mix well, then simmer for 10 minutes until the liquid has been absorbed and the orzo is cooked through, stirring now and then. Stir in the cream and cook for a further minute.

To serve, scatter the crispy chorizo and bacon on top, then finish with grated Parmesan, parsley, and black pepper.

KCAL	CARBS	PROTEIN	FAT
545	48G	33G	24G

Lasagne loaded fries

Prep 5 mins
Cook 20 mins
Serves 2
Freeze (Bolognese only)

If you know me, you'll know that I love anything lasagne-related; I think it's an addiction. Here, crispy fries are loaded with Bolognese sauce and béchamel, then topped with mozzarella. It's beyond delicious.

280g (9½oz) shop-bought skin-on fries
spray oil
½ onion, finely diced
4 mushrooms, finely diced
250g (9oz) lean beef mince (ground beef)
250ml (1 cup plus 1 tbsp/9fl oz) beef stock
250g (9oz) passata
1 tsp mixed herbs
pinch of garlic granules
good pinch of freshly ground black pepper
pinch of granulated sugar
1 bay leaf
80g (2¾oz) shop-bought béchamel sauce
40g (1¼oz) grated mozzarella
1 tbsp grated Parmesan
pinch of dried parsley (optional)

Cook the fries according to the packet instructions.

Meanwhile, spray a large frying pan with oil, then add the onion and mushrooms. Fry over a medium heat for a few minutes to soften, then add the beef mince and fry for a further few minutes until browned. Stir in the stock, passata, mixed herbs, garlic granules, black pepper, sugar, and bay leaf. Mix well and simmer for 8–10 minutes, or until the liquid has evaporated, then remove the bay leaf. This is your Bolognese sauce.

Tip the cooked fries into an ovenproof dish, then scoop over the Bolognese sauce. Top with the béchamel sauce, followed by the mozzarella and Parmesan. Air-fry at 190°C (375°F) for 4–5 minutes until the cheese has melted. Alternatively, cook in an oven preheated to 200°C (180°C fan/400°F/Gas 6) for 10–15 minutes.

Top with a sprinkling of dried parsley, if you like, then serve and enjoy.

KCAL	CARBS	PROTEIN	FAT
599	56G	40G	24G

Smash & stack burger

Prep 5 mins
Cook 6-7 mins
Serves 2

Inspired by everyone's favourite fast-food burger, but my version is lower in calories and higher in protein. It also tastes even better ... in my opinion.

250g (9oz) lean beef mince (ground beef)
spray oil
4 cheese singles
2 seeded burger buns
80g (2¾oz) iceberg lettuce, sliced
1 gherkin (pickle), sliced
20g (¾oz) onion, finely diced
½ portion Homemade Fries (see page 109)
salt and freshly ground black pepper

For the sauce
3 tbsp light mayonnaise
1 tbsp tomato ketchup
1 tsp English mustard
1 tbsp pickle juice (from the gherkin jar)
pinch of paprika
pinch of garlic granules

Combine the sauce ingredients in a bowl and mix well, then set aside in the refrigerator.

Divide the beef mince into 4 even-sized portions. Roll into balls, then press down to form thick patties (see tip). Season with salt and pepper, then spray with oil and air-fry at 200°C (390°F) for 6 minutes, adding a cheese slice to each patty 1 minute before the end of the cooking time.

Alternatively, spray a large frying pan with oil and place over a high heat. Add the patties and flatten them as much as you can, pressing them down into the pan with a spatula. Season with salt and pepper, then fry for 3–4 minutes until the base of each patty has a lovely, caramelized crust. Flip, then cook for a further 1 minute on the other side. Add a cheese slice to each patty, then turn off the heat and leave them in the pan for a few minutes more to allow the cheese to melt.

Lightly toast your burger buns, then assemble by spreading some of the burger sauce on the bottom half of each bun, followed by some lettuce, a burger patty, some more lettuce, another burger patty, and then some more sauce. Finish with the gherkin and onion, then place the top half of the burger buns on top. Serve with the fries.

TIP If you're using the air-fryer method, make the patties nice and thick so they don't dry out!

KCAL	CARBS	PROTEIN	FAT
599	71G	45G	15G

Sweet chilli fish finger tacos

Prep 5 mins
Cook 10 mins
Serves 2
Freeze (fish fingers)

If you fancy switching it up from your usual meat recipes, try this bad boy. Sweet chilli sauce drizzled over crispy battered fish fingers and served on soft white tortilla tacos.

3 tbsp light mayonnaise
4 tbsp reduced-sugar sweet chilli sauce
250g (9oz) skinless cod fillets
1 tsp paprika
2 garlic cloves, minced
25g (scant 1oz) panko breadcrumbs
pinch of salt
4 mini tortilla wraps
100g (3½oz) iceberg lettuce, sliced
10g (¼oz) pickled red onions (see tip on page 93), to serve

Mix the mayonnaise with 2 tablespoons of the sweet chilli sauce, and split this mixture between two bowls, reserving one for later on.

Cut the cod fillets into fish finger-sized pieces, about four pieces per fillet, then season with the paprika and minced garlic. Dip the cod pieces into one of the sauce bowls, then dip them in the breadcrumbs, turning to coat. Air-fry at 190°C (375°F) for 10 minutes or until cooked through. Alternatively, cook in an oven preheated to 180°C (160°C fan/350°F/Gas 4) for 15 minutes. Season the cooked fish fingers with a pinch of salt.

Toast the mini tortillas under a hot grill (broiler) or in the air fryer for a few minutes to crisp up, then spread the reserved sweet chilli mayo over each tortilla.

Top with the sliced lettuce, followed by the fish fingers. Serve topped with pickled onions, and drizzled with the remaining sweet chilli sauce.

KCAL	CARBS	PROTEIN	FAT
409	53G	34G	6G

Creamy Tuscan turkey meatballs

Prep 5-10 mins
Cook 18-20 mins
Serves 4
Freeze

Beautifully seasoned turkey meatballs in the most glorious Tuscan cream sauce. I always make double so I can enjoy these all week. I love them.

500g (1lb 2oz) lean turkey mince (ground turkey)
1 tsp paprika
4 garlic cloves, minced
50g (1¾oz) breadcrumbs (I used panko)
40g (1¼oz) Parmesan, grated
spray oil
½ onion, finely diced
65g (2¼oz) sun-dried tomatoes, drained and sliced
5–6 basil leaves, sliced, plus 3 stalks, finely diced
150ml (⅔ cup/5fl oz) chicken stock
80ml (2¾fl oz) single (half and half) cream
2 tbsp low-fat red pesto (or use sun-dried tomato paste)
squeeze of lemon juice
salt and freshly ground black pepper

In a bowl, combine the turkey mince with the paprika, minced garlic, breadcrumbs, and half the grated Parmesan. Season with salt and pepper and mix well to combine.

Roll into 16 equal-sized balls, spray with oil and air-fry at 190°C (375°F) for 8–10 minutes, shaking halfway. Alternatively, spray a large frying pan with oil, then add the meatballs and fry over a medium heat for 10–12 minutes until golden.

To make the sauce, spray a large frying pan with oil and add the onion. Fry over a medium heat for a few minutes to soften, then add the sun-dried tomatoes and basil stalks. Fry for a further minute before adding the chicken stock, cream, red pesto, and remaining Parmesan. Mix well, then add the cooked meatballs and simmer for 5–6 minutes or until the meatballs are fully cooked through.

Squeeze over the lemon and scatter over the basil leaves to serve.

TIP Serve with any type of pasta – or with creamy mash and Tenderstem broccoli.

KCAL	CARBS	PROTEIN	FAT
328	13G	39G	13G

Sticky paprika halloumi gyros

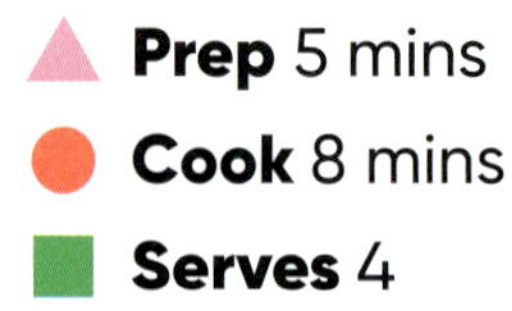

Being Greek-Cypriot, we have gyros at home very, very regularly. As I've shared gyros recipes in my other cookbooks, here's a twist for you: sticky paprika-flavoured grilled halloumi, stuffed inside a pitta with fries and salad.

160g (5¾oz) shop-bought skin-on fries
25g (scant 1oz) honey
squeeze of lemon juice
420g (14¾oz) low-fat halloumi, sliced
spray oil
2 tsp paprika
4 pitta breads or flatbreads
2 tomatoes, sliced
20g (¾oz) red onion, sliced

For the tzatziki
150g (5½oz) cucumber, grated
200g (7oz) fat-free Greek yogurt
juice of ½ lemon
2 garlic cloves, minced
1 tsp olive oil
salt and freshly ground black pepper

Cook the skin-on fries according to the packet instructions.

Meanwhile, prepare the tzatziki. Squeeze the grated cucumber to remove as much liquid as possible, then add to a bowl with the remaining tzatziki ingredients. Mix well and set aside in the fridge.

In another bowl, combine the honey and lemon. Set aside.

Spray the halloumi with oil and scatter over the paprika. Air-fry at 200°C (390°F) without the crisper plate for 6 minutes, then pour in the honey-and-lemon mixture and air-fry for 2 minutes more at 220°C (430°F) until wonderfully sticky. Take care not to overcrowd the fryer – work in batches or use the second drawer if you have one. Alternatively, spray a large frying pan with oil and fry the halloumi over a high heat for 4 minutes until golden, then flip and cook for a further minute or two on the other side. Pour over the honey-and-lemon mixture, and fry for 1 minute more until lovely and sticky.

Lightly toast the pitta breads, then spread each one with the tzatziki. Pile on the tomatoes, onion, halloumi, and fries, and serve.

TIP Sometimes I like to change it up and use smoked paprika!

KCAL	CARBS	PROTEIN	FAT
581	56G	37G	23G

Salmon tikka skewers with garlic naan

Prep 5 mins
Cook 8 mins
Serves 4
Freeze (salmon only)

I'm a big fan of flavouring meat with tikka curry paste, so I thought I'd try it on salmon – and it works brilliantly. Here, I serve it on garlic naan, with an easy-peasy mint yogurt and onion salad.

4 skinless salmon fillets
50g (1¾oz) tikka curry paste
spray oil

For the onion salad
3 tomatoes, deseeded and finely diced
¼ onion, finely diced
⅓ cucumber, finely diced
1–2 coriander (cilantro) sprigs, finely chopped
juice of ½ lemon, plus extra to serve

For the mint yogurt
2 tsp mint sauce
4 heaped tbsp fat-free Greek yogurt

For the garlic naans
1 tbsp low-fat butter
2 garlic cloves, minced
1 tsp dried parsley
4 shop-bought mini naans

Slice each salmon fillet into 4 big chunks, then coat with the tikka curry paste. Thread on to skewers, spray with oil and air-fry at 190°C (375°F) for 6–8 minutes. Alternatively, spray a frying pan with oil and fry the salmon skewers over a medium heat for a couple of minutes on all 4 sides.

Meanwhile, combine all the onion salad ingredients in a bowl and toss to combine. In a separate bowl, combine the mint sauce and yogurt, adding a dash of cold water to loosen.

For the garlic naans, heat the butter and garlic in a small bowl in the microwave for 10–15 seconds, or until the butter has melted. Stir in the dried parsley, then brush the mixture over the mini naans. Grill (broil) on high for a few minutes, or air-fry at 190°C (375°F) for 3–4 minutes until toasted.

Serve all the components together so people can build their own mini naans. I like to load up my naan with a salmon skewer and some onion salad, then drizzle mint yogurt over the top and finish with a squeeze of lemon.

KCAL	CARBS	PROTEIN	FAT
448	28G	31G	23G

Enchiladas with a crushed tortilla crumb

Prep 5 mins
Cook 15–20 mins
Serves 4
Freeze

This is such an easy recipe, incorporating some seriously tasty flavours. Sliced tortillas are stirred into a homemade enchilada sauce until soft, then finished with an array of toppings and a crunchy tortilla crumb for serious texture.

1 onion, finely diced
1 red (bell) pepper, finely diced
500g (1lb 2oz) lean beef mince (ground beef)
2 tbsp taco seasoning
2 tbsp tomato purée
200g (7oz) canned sweetcorn
500g (1lb 2oz) passata
150ml (⅔ cup/5fl oz) beef stock
1 tsp Worcestershire sauce
3 mini tortilla wraps, sliced into strips
40g (1¼oz) grated mozzarella
60g (2oz) low-fat Cheddar, grated
spray oil (optional)
salt and freshly ground black pepper

To serve
freshly chopped coriander (cilantro)
4 tbsp low-fat sour cream
30g (1oz) tortilla chips, crushed

Add the onion and red pepper to the air fryer without the crisper plate, then add the beef mince on top. Use a spatula to break up the mince, then air-fry at 200°C (390°F) for 3 minutes. Give it all a good mix, then stir in the taco seasoning, and season with salt and pepper. Air-fry for a further 5 minutes, then add the tomato purée, sweetcorn, passata, beef stock, and Worcestershire sauce. Submerge the strips of tortilla in the mixture, scatter the mozzarella and Cheddar over the top, and air-fry for 5–7 minutes more until the cheese has melted.

Alternatively, spray a large, lidded frying pan with oil. Add the onion and red pepper and fry over a medium heat for a few minutes to soften. Add the beef mince and fry for 3–4 minutes until browned, then stir in the taco seasoning and tomato purée. Season with salt and pepper, then stir in the sweetcorn, passata, beef stock, and Worcestershire sauce, before submerging the strips of tortilla in the mixture. Scatter over both cheeses, then cover the pan with a lid and simmer for 8–10 minutes until the cheese has melted and the sauce has soaked into the tortilla wraps.

Serve topped with fresh coriander, dollops of sour cream, and the crushed tortilla chips for crunch.

KCAL	CARBS	PROTEIN	FAT
484	44G	41G	17G

Chicken & pepperoni pizza wraps

Prep 5 mins
Cook 17–19 mins
Serves 2
Freeze

All the banging pizza flavours inside (and outside) a tortilla wrap, folded and air-fried until cheesy and crispy. A recipe the whole family will adore.

- 250g (9oz) chicken breast, butterflied
- 1 tsp Italian seasoning
- spray oil
- 1 small onion, finely diced
- ⅓ red (bell) pepper, finely diced
- 35g (1¼oz) tomato purée
- 170g (5¾oz) passata
- 1 tsp dried oregano
- ½ tsp garlic granules
- 2 tortilla wraps
- 30g (1oz) grated mozzarella
- 4 pepperoni slices
- salt and freshly ground black pepper

Season the chicken with salt, pepper, and Italian seasoning. Spray a frying pan with oil, then add the chicken and fry over a medium–high heat for 3 minutes on each side or until nearly cooked. Remove from the pan and set aside to rest.

Spray the pan with more oil, then add the onion and pepper and fry over a medium heat for a few minutes to soften. Stir in half the tomato purée, along with the passata, oregano, and garlic granules. Dice the chicken, then stir it into your pizza sauce.

Take off the heat and allow the mixture to cool slightly before dividing it between the tortilla wraps. Roll up the wraps and place on a lined baking tray. Spread the remaining tomato purée on top of the wraps, then sprinkle over the mozzarella, pressing it down so it sticks to the tomato purée. Finally, add 2 pepperoni slices to the top of each wraps, using a toothpick to keep them in place (mine usually blow away if I don't do this!). Air-fry at 190°C (375°F) for 5–7 minutes until the cheese is melted and golden. Alternatively, cook in an oven preheated to 200°C (180°C fan/400°F/Gas 6) for 8–10 minutes.

Serve and enjoy.

KCAL	CARBS	PROTEIN	FAT
452	41G	43G	12G

Mini Kyiv bites & creamy mash

Prep 5–10 mins
Cook 15 mins
Serves 4
Freeze

I love a chicken Kyiv, but they can be a lot of effort to make. So I made these mini ones, which are simplified by drizzling the garlic butter over the top.

70g (2¼oz) panko breadcrumbs
2 tsp garlic granules
2 tsp mixed herbs
500g (1lb 2oz) chicken mince (ground chicken), or use finely diced chicken breast
1 egg, whisked
spray oil
300g (10oz) green beans
salt and freshly ground black pepper

For the creamy mash
800g (1¾lb) potatoes, diced into small chunks
2 tbsp low-fat butter
200ml (scant 1 cup/7fl oz) semi-skimmed milk

For the garlic butter
3 tbsp low-fat butter
2–3 garlic cloves, minced
1 heaped tsp freshly chopped parsley

In a shallow bowl, combine the panko breadcrumbs with 1 teaspoon each of the garlic granules and mixed herbs.

Season the chicken with a good pinch of salt and pepper, then stir in the remaining 1 teaspoon each of the garlic granules and mixed herbs. Wet your hands and roll the chicken into 16 bite-sized balls. Dip each ball into the whisked egg, then coat in the seasoned panko breadcrumbs.

Spray the chicken balls with oil and air-fry at 190°C (375°F) for 7 minutes, then turn over, spray again and air-fry for a further 5 minutes until cooked through. Use the crisper tray, and work in batches if needed. Alternatively, arrange the chicken balls on a lined baking tray, spray with oil, and cook in an oven preheated to 190°C (170°C fan/375°F/Gas 5) for 18–20 minutes, turning halfway.

Meanwhile, for the mash, bring a saucepan of water to the boil, add the potatoes, and boil for 15 minutes until tender. Drain and mash until smooth, then stir in the butter and milk until creamy. Season with salt and pepper to taste. In a separate pan, blanch the green beans for 3 minutes, then drain.

To make the garlic butter, heat the butter and garlic in a small bowl in the microwave for 10–15 seconds, or until the butter has melted, then stir in the dried parsley.

Serve the chicken bites, green beans and creamy mash with the garlic butter drizzled over the top.

KCAL	CARBS	PROTEIN	FAT
525	55G	35G	18G

Philly cheesesteaks

Prep 5 mins
Cook 15 mins
Serves 2

Packed with steak, melted cheese, sautéed onions, and peppers, and dipped into a homemade cheese sauce, these rolls are comfort food at its finest.

300g (10oz) lean rump steak (or any lean cut)
spray oil
½ onion, finely diced
½ green (bell) pepper, diced
1 tsp smoked paprika
1 tsp garlic granules
½ beef stock cube
2 × 45g (1½oz) brioche hotdog rolls or submarine rolls, opened
30g (1oz) grated mozzarella
salt and freshly ground black pepper

For the garlic butter
2 tsp low-fat butter
1 garlic clove, minced
pinch of dried parsley

For the cheesy sauce
2 cheese singles
1 tbsp semi-skimmed (2 per cent) milk

Season the steak with salt and pepper, then spray with oil. Heat a frying pan over a medium heat. Add the steak and fry for 2 minutes on either side (for medium–rare). Remove from the pan and set aside to rest.

Spray the same pan with oil, and fry the onion and pepper over a high heat for a few minutes to char, then reduce the heat to low–medium. Slice the steak into thin strips and add to the pan, along with any resting juices. Add the paprika and garlic granules, then crumble in the stock cube. Add a dash of boiling water and mix well.

To make the garlic butter, heat the butter and garlic in a small bowl in the microwave for 10–15 seconds, or until the butter has melted, then stir in the dried parsley.

Fill the rolls with the steak, pepper, and onion. Scatter over the mozzarella, then brush with the garlic butter.

Air-fry at 180°C (350°F) for 3–5 minutes until the cheese is bubbly. Alternatively, cook in an oven preheated to 180°C (160°C fan/350°F/Gas 4) for 8–10 minutes.

Meanwhile, combine the cheese slices and milk in a mug or small bowl and microwave in 10-second bursts, stirring well between each burst, until you have a cheesy sauce.

Serve the rolls with the sauce drizzled over the top.

KCAL	CARBS	PROTEIN	FAT
477	31G	46G	18G

Beef satay skewers with zingy slaw

Satay sauce is my absolute favourite – not only is it completely delicious, but it's also high in protein! Drizzle it over beef skewers, and serve with zingy slaw to get your veggies in.

225g (8oz) microwaveable sticky rice (or use precooked rice)
300g (10oz) lean rump steak
1 tbsp soy sauce
1 tsp curry powder
2 tsp rice vinegar
1 heaped tbsp cornflour (cornstarch)
spray oil

For the satay sauce
20g (¾oz) peanut butter (crunchy or smooth)
1 tbsp soy sauce
1 tsp honey
1 tsp shop-bought ginger purée (or freshly grated ginger)

For the slaw
40g (1¼oz) red cabbage, finely shredded
1 carrot, finely shredded
2 spring onions (green onions), sliced
a few dashes of fish sauce
juice of ½ lime
1 tsp honey

In a bowl, combine the satay sauce ingredients with 2 tablespoons boiling water. Mix well and set aside. In a separate bowl, combine the slaw ingredients, then mix well and set aside.

Prepare the sticky rice according to the packet instructions.

Tenderize the steak with a tenderizer or cover with cling film (plastic wrap) and bash with a rolling pin. Slice it into thin slices, working against the grain. Place in a bowl with the soy sauce, curry powder, and rice vinegar, and stir to coat. Dust with the cornflour, then thread the beef on to skewers. Spray with oil and air-fry at 200°C (390°F) for 5–6 minutes (this will cook it medium–rare), then leave to rest for a few minutes. Alternatively, grill (broil) the steak skewers on medium–high for 3 minutes on each side, or until cooked to your liking.

Serve with the sticky rice and slaw, then drizzle over your delicious homemade satay sauce.

KCAL	CARBS	PROTEIN	FAT
536	65G	41G	12G

Supercharged chicken tower burger

Prep 5 mins
Cook 13–15 mins
Serves 2
Freeze (chicken only)

There's no denying the deliciousness of a fried chicken burger with zingy sauce. Next time the craving hits, here's a healthy version you'll love.

2 × 110g (4oz) chicken breasts
2 tsp paprika
1 tsp garlic granules
1 egg white, whisked
30g (1oz) spicy tortilla chips, crushed
2 shop-bought frozen hash browns
2 low-fat cheese singles
2 seeded brioche buns
40g (1¼oz) iceberg lettuce, sliced
salt and freshly ground black pepper

For the supercharged sauce
3 tbsp low-fat mayonnaise
1 tsp sriracha
2 tsp tomato ketchup
½ tsp rice wine vinegar
½ tsp Dijon mustard
½ tsp paprika
½ tsp garlic granules

In a small bowl, combine the sauce ingredients with 1–2 tablespoons cold water. Mix well and set aside in the refrigerator.

Season the chicken breasts with salt and pepper, and scatter over the paprika and garlic granules. Tip the crushed tortilla chips into a shallow bowl. Dip each chicken breast into the whisked egg white, then into the crushed tortilla chips to coat. Air-fry the coated chicken breasts and hash browns at 190°C (375°F) for 12–14 minutes, flipping everything halfway. Turn off the air fryer, then top each chicken breast with a cheese slice and leave to melt in the residual heat. Alternatively, cook the chicken breasts and hash browns in an oven preheated to 200°C (180°C fan/400°F/Gas 6) for 20 minutes, adding the cheese slices for the last minute or two.

Lightly toast the brioche buns, then assemble by spreading some of the burger sauce on the bottom half of each bun. Top with the lettuce, followed by the chicken breasts and hash browns. Drizzle over any remaining sauce, then place the top half of the burger buns on top and dive in.

TIP Serve with my Homemade Fries (see page 109).

KCAL	CARBS	PROTEIN	FAT
479	44G	40G	15G

Loaded bacon cheeseburger mac & cheese

Prep 5 mins
Cook 20 mins
Serves 4
Freeze

One of my favourite mac-and-cheese recipes, and a great one to meal prep! All your favourite burger flavours, plus creamy mac and cheese.

200g (7oz) macaroni
4 smoked streaky bacon rashers (slices)
spray oil
1 onion, finely diced
500g (1lb 2oz) lean beef mince (ground beef)
1 tsp paprika
1 tsp garlic granules
1 tsp English mustard
200g (7oz) canned chopped tomatoes
a few dashes of Worcestershire sauce
1 beef stock cube
60g (2oz) low-fat Cheddar, grated
salt and freshly ground black pepper

For the burger sauce
3 tbsp low-fat mayonnaise
1 heaped tbsp tomato ketchup
1 tsp English mustard
pinch of garlic granules
pinch of paprika
dash of pickle juice (from a jar of gherkins/pickles)

Cook the macaroni according to the packet instructions, then drain and set aside.

Air-fry the bacon at 200°C (390°F) for 4 minutes until crisp. Alternatively, grill (broil) on high for 6–8 minutes. Dice and set aside.

Mix together the burger sauce ingredients, then set aside.

Spray a large pan with oil and fry the onion over a medium heat for a few minutes to soften. Add the beef and fry for a few minutes more. Season with salt and pepper, then add the paprika, garlic granules, mustard, chopped tomatoes, and Worcestershire sauce. Crumble in the stock cube and add a dash of boiling water, then stir. Cook for a few minutes until the mixture thickens, then stir in the macaroni.

Transfer into an ovenproof dish and scatter the grated cheese over the top. Air-fry at 200°C (390°F) for 5–8 minutes until the cheese has melted and has a lovely colour. Alternatively, cook in an oven preheated to 200°C (180°C fan/400°F/Gas 6) for 15–20 minutes.

Just before serving, drizzle your homemade burger sauce over the top, then scatter over the crispy bacon bits.

KCAL	CARBS	PROTEIN	FAT
484	46G	42G	15G

Hoisin beef taco pancakes

Prep 5 mins
Cook 6 mins
Serves 2
Freeze (beef only)

I love duck pancakes, but they're a bit too easy to devour – I could just shovel them down and suddenly realize I'd demolished ten. This recipe uses a filling, sticky hoisin beef instead. I promise you, you won't be looking back.

250g (9oz) lean beef mince (ground beef)
1 heaped tsp five-spice powder
spray oil
3 tbsp hoisin sauce, plus extra to serve
1 tsp dark soy sauce
4 mini tortilla wraps
½ cucumber, sliced into matchsticks
2 spring onions (green onions), sliced into matchsticks
sesame seeds, for sprinkling
salt and freshly ground black pepper

Season the beef mince with the five-spice powder and spray with oil. Air-fry without the crisper plate at 200°C (390°F) for 5 minutes. Break up the mince with a spatula, then stir in the hoisin and soy sauce, ensuring the beef is fully coated in the sauce. Air-fry for a further 1 minute.

Alternatively, spray a frying pan with oil and place over a high heat. Add the beef mince and season with five-spice powder. Fry for 4–5 minutes until browned, then stir in the hoisin sauce and soy sauce. Cook for a further couple of minutes until the beef goes dark and sticky.

When you're ready to serve, microwave the mini tortilla wraps for 10 seconds to warm through.

I like to eat mine by piling the beef on to a wrap, then topping with cucumber, spring onion, and a cheeky drizzle of hoisin sauce. Sprinkle with a few sesame seeds to finish, and then all you need to do is roll up and enjoy.

KCAL	CARBS	PROTEIN	FAT
408	46G	32G	9G

Cheesy chicken chipotle rice

Prep 10 mins
Cook 15 mins
Serves 2
Freeze

If you're craving chipotle flavours, then this recipe has everything you could ask for. It's zingy, smoky, and completely delicious.

- juice of ½ lime
- 1 tsp chipotle paste
- 1 tsp honey
- 250g (9oz) chicken breast, butterflied
- ½ red onion, finely diced
- 60g (2oz) canned sweetcorn
- spray oil
- 100g (3½oz) canned black beans, drained
- 1 heaped tbsp tomato purée
- 200g (7oz) canned chopped tomatoes
- 1 tbsp taco seasoning
- 1 chicken stock cube
- 250g (9oz) pouch microwaveable Mexican-style rice (or use precooked rice)
- 30g (1oz) low-fat Cheddar, grated
- fresh coriander (cilantro), to serve

For the chipotle sauce

- juice of ½ lime
- 1 tsp chipotle paste
- 1 tsp honey
- 50g (1¾oz) sour cream

In a small bowl, mix together the chipotle sauce ingredients, then set aside.

In another bowl, combine the lime juice, chipotle paste, and honey. Add the chicken and stir to coat, then air-fry at 190°C (375°F) for 8 minutes without the crisper plate. Remove and set aside. Add the onion and sweetcorn to the air fryer, spray with oil, and air-fry at 200°C (390°F) for 3–4 minutes. Add the black beans, tomato purée, chopped tomatoes, taco seasoning, and stock cube, along with a dash of boiling water, then stir in the rice (no need to microwave it). Slice the chicken (it won't yet be fully cooked) and arrange it on top, then sprinkle over the cheese. Air-fry at 200°C (390°F) for 4–6 minutes until the cheese has melted and all the liquid has been soaked up.

Alternatively, spray an ovenproof frying pan with oil and fry the chicken over a medium heat for 4 minutes on each side, then remove from the pan and set aside. In the same pan, fry the onion for a few minutes to soften, then add the sweetcorn. Increase the heat to high and fry for a few minutes to char. Add the black beans, tomato purée, chopped tomatoes, taco seasoning, stock cube, dash of boiling water, and rice as above, and mix well. Cook for a few minutes until the rice has softened, then slice the chicken and add on top. Sprinkle over the cheese, then grill (broil) on high for 3 minutes to melt.

To serve, drizzle with the creamy chipotle sauce and scatter over some fresh coriander to finish.

KCAL	CARBS	PROTEIN	FAT
575	67G	46G	12G

WITH A LITTLE BIT OF MEAL PREP, YOU CAN JUST HEAT, EAT AND ENJOY! THESE PREP-AHEAD ‘READY MEALS’ ARE PERFECT TO MAKE ON A SUNDAY, THEN STORE IN THE FRIDGE TO EAT THROUGHOUT THE WEEK.

MEAL-PREPPED & READY TO GO

Cajun-spiced BBQ-honey burrito bowl

Prep 5 mins
Cook 5–6 mins
Serves 2

When you want a delicious meal without much effort, a burrito bowl is the way to go. Packed with different elements to keep you satisfied, while making every mouthful a treat.

250g (9oz) pouch microwaveable Mexican-style rice (or use precooked rice)
260g (9¼oz) chicken breast, diced
2½ tsp Cajun seasoning
oil spray
1 tsp honey
1½ tbsp barbecue sauce
50g (1¾oz) flatbread, cut into triangles
salt and freshly ground black pepper

For the sauce
2 tbsp low-fat mayonnaise
1 heaped tbsp barbecue sauce
1 tsp Cajun seasoning

For the salad
45g (1½oz) canned sweetcorn
80g (2¾oz) iceberg lettuce, sliced
20g (¾oz) red onion, finely diced
8 cherry tomatoes, diced

In a bowl, mix together the sauce ingredients with 1 tablespoon water, then set aside. Prepare the rice according to the packet instructions and set aside.

Season the diced chicken with salt and pepper, along with 1½ teaspoons of the Cajun seasoning. Spray with oil and air-fry at 200°C (390°F) for 7–8 minutes or until cooked through. Drizzle over the honey and barbecue sauce and air-fry for a further minute. Alternatively, spray a frying pan with oil and fry the chicken over a high heat for 2 minutes to get a lovely char on the meat, then reduce the heat to medium and flip to cook on the other side for a further 4–6 minutes or until cooked through. Drizzle over the barbecue sauce and honey, increase the heat to high, and cook for 1 minute more.

Spray the flatbread triangles with oil, season with the remaining 1 teaspoon Cajun seasoning, and air-fry at 200°C (390°F) for 3–4 minutes. Alternatively, cook in an oven preheated to 200°C (180°C fan/400°F/Gas 6) for 5–10 minutes.

Combine the salad ingredients in a large bowl and toss, then divide between 2 bowls, along with the rice, chicken, and flatbread triangles. Serve with the sauce.

KCAL	CARBS	PROTEIN	FAT
512	64G	40G	8G

Chicken & feta meatball wellness bowl

Prep 10 mins
Cook 10–12 mins
Serves 4
Freeze (meatballs only)

This Greek-themed wellness bowl has everything you could want and more. Those chicken-and-feta meatballs are to die for!

500g (1lb 2oz) chicken mince (ground chicken)
1 egg
60g (2oz) feta, crumbled
50g (1¾oz) panko breadcrumbs
1 small red onion, finely diced
2 garlic cloves, minced
1 tbsp finely chopped dill
2 tsp dried oregano
spray oil
80g (2¾oz) flatbread, cut into triangles
1 tsp paprika
10 cherry tomatoes, diced
100g (3½oz) cucumber, diced
40g (1¼oz) pickled red onions (see below)
1 portion Tzatziki (see page 66)
lemon wedges, for squeezing
salt and freshly ground black pepper

TIP To make your own pickled red onions, mix onion slices with 1 tbsp red wine vinegar and a pinch of sugar and leave for 20 minutes.

In a large bowl, combine the chicken mince, egg, feta, breadcrumbs, diced onion, garlic, dill, and oregano. Season with a good pinch of salt and pepper and mix well. Divide into 16 equal-sized portions and roll into meatballs.

Spray the meatballs with oil and air-fry at 190°C (375°F) for 10–12 minutes or until cooked through, shaking halfway. Take care not to overcrowd the fryer – work in batches or use the second drawer if you have one. Alternatively, spray a large frying pan with oil and place over a medium heat. Fry the meatballs for 12–14 minutes until cooked through.

Meanwhile, spray the flatbread triangles with oil and season with salt, pepper, and the paprika. Air-fry at 200°C (390°F) for 3–4 minutes until crispy, or cook in an oven preheated to 200°C (180°C fan/400°F/Gas 6) for 5–10 minutes.

Divide the tomatoes and cucumber between 2 bowls, followed by the meatballs, pickled onions, and toasted flatbread. Serve with a dollop of tzatziki and a good squeeze of lemon over the meatballs.

KCAL	CARBS	PROTEIN	FAT
521	65G	41G	12G

Crispy sweet Buffalo chicken Caesar salad with skin-on fries

Prep 5 mins
Cook 14 mins
Serves 2
Freeze (chicken only)

You probably all know how to make a Caesar salad, but I wanted to share my own twist, with a hot honey glaze over the crispy chicken to complement the creamy Caesar dressing.

250g (9oz) chicken breast, butterflied
1 tsp paprika
1 tsp garlic granules
1 egg, whisked
30g (1oz) cornflakes, crushed
120g (4¼oz) shop-bought skin-on fries
2 handfuls of romaine lettuce, sliced
100g (3½oz) shop-bought low-fat Caesar dressing
10g (¼oz) Parmesan, grated
salt and freshly ground black pepper

For the Buffalo sauce
1 tsp honey
1 tbsp reduced-sugar sweet chilli sauce
1 tsp hot sauce
pinch of chilli flakes

Season the chicken with the paprika and garlic granules, along with some salt and pepper. Dip into the whisked egg, then the crushed cornflakes, turning to coat. Air-fry the coated chicken and the fries at 190°C (375°F) for 12–14 minutes, turning the chicken halfway. Once the chicken is cooked through, remove it from the air fryer, and give the fries a further 5 minutes if needed. Alternatively, cook the fries and chicken in an oven preheated to 200°C (180°C fan/400°F/Gas 6) for 20 minutes. Slice the cooked chicken into strips.

Meanwhile, in a bowl, mix together the Buffalo sauce ingredients.

In a large bowl, mix the romaine lettuce with the Caesar dressing. Divide between 2 plates, and scatter over the grated Parmesan. Top with the fries and sliced crispy chicken, then drizzle over the sauce and serve.

KCAL	CARBS	PROTEIN	FAT
436	37G	45G	11G

Creamy cheesy sausage gnocchi

Prep 5 mins
Cook 10 mins
Serves 2
Freeze

Pillowy gnocchi mixed with a beautiful sausage ragu, served with a garlic flatbread to mop up all the juices. If you don't fancy gnocchi, you can swap it for any pasta your heart (or belly) desires.

280g (9½oz) gnocchi
1 small red onion, finely diced
6 low-fat sausages, skins removed
spray oil
25g (scant 1oz) tomato purée
2 garlic cloves, minced
55ml (2fl oz) single (half and half) cream
1 chicken stock cube
40g (1¼oz) low-fat Cheddar, grated
10g (¼oz) Parmesan, grated
salt and freshly ground black pepper
freshly chopped parsley, to serve

Cook the gnocchi according to the packet instructions, then drain, reserving 1 ladleful of the cooking water.

Add the onion and sausage meat to the air fryer without the crisper plate, breaking up the meat with your hands. Spray with oil and air-fry at 200°C (390°F) for 5–6 minutes, stirring halfway and further breaking up the sausage meat. Stir in the tomato purée, garlic, and cream, then crumble over the stock cube. Add the reserved gnocchi water and stir to combine, then add the gnocchi. Top with the grated cheeses. Air-fry for a further 1–2 minutes to melt the cheese.

Alternatively, spray a frying pan with oil and place over a medium heat. Fry the onions for a few minutes to soften, then add the sausage meat and fry for 4–5 minutes or until crispy. Mix in the tomato purée and garlic, then pour in the cream. Crumble in the stock cube and stir in the reserved cooking water. Lastly, stir in the grated cheese and gnocchi, mixing well.

Season with black pepper and scatter over the parsley to serve.

TIPS This is delicious with garlic bread.

If you choose the frying pan method, reserve some of the crispy sausage to sprinkle over the top at the end.

KCAL	CARBS	PROTEIN	FAT
590	63G	34G	20G

Crispy bacon bits burger salad

Prep 5 mins
Cook 5–6 mins
Serves 4

I could eat this salad every day and never get bored. All the joy of eating a burger while still getting in plenty of veggies.

4 streaky bacon rashers (slices)
500g (1lb 2oz) lean beef mince (ground beef)
spray oil
1 beef stock cube
2 tsp English mustard
40g (1¼oz) tomato purée
200g (7oz) iceberg lettuce, sliced
20 cherry tomatoes, diced
80g (2¾oz) low-fat Cheddar, grated
2 gherkins (pickles), sliced
1 tsp sesame seeds

For the smoky burger sauce
60g (2oz) low-fat mayonnaise
2 tbsp tomato ketchup
2 tsp English mustard
1 tsp smoked paprika
1 tsp garlic granules
dash of pickle juice (from the gherkin/pickle jar)

TIP If you can find bacon-flavour salad sprinkles or crumbles, sprinkle them on to the salad for extra flavour and crunch.

In a bowl, mix together all the sauce ingredients and set aside in the refrigerator.

Air-fry the bacon at 200°C (390°F) for 4 minutes or until crispy. Alternatively, grill (broil) on high for 6–8 minutes. Let the bacon cool, then dice and set aside.

Add the beef mince to the air fryer without the crisper plate, gently breaking it into big chunks using a spatula. Spray with oil and air-fry at 200°C (390°F) for 5 minutes, stirring halfway. Crumble in the stock cube, then stir in the mustard, tomato purée, and a dash of boiling water. Mix well and air-fry for a further 1–2 minutes. Alternatively, spray a frying pan with oil and fry the beef mince over a medium heat for 5–6 minutes until browned, then crumble in the stock cube. Add the mustard, tomato purée, and a dash of boiling water. Mix well and cook for 2 minutes more.

To assemble, divide the lettuce and tomatoes between 4 bowls. Add the beef mixture, then top with the cheese and gherkins. Sprinkle with the sesame seeds, then finish with the diced bacon and serve with the sauce.

KCAL	CARBS	PROTEIN	FAT
331	10G	40G	14G

Chicken fried rice with bang bang sauce

Prep 5–10 mins
Cook 14 mins
Serves 2
Freeze

I could drizzle bang bang sauce on just about anything, and I swear it would never get old. This chicken fried rice gets 10 out of 10. Every. Single. Time.

300g (10oz) chicken breast, cut into bite-sized chunks
1 tsp soy sauce
1 garlic clove, minced
2.5cm (1in) piece of fresh ginger, minced
25g (scant 1oz) cornflour (cornstarch)
spray oil
250g (9oz) pouch microwaveable long-grain rice (or use precooked rice)
1 carrot, grated
100g (3½oz) frozen peas
1 tsp dark soy sauce
2 tbsp reduced-sugar sweet chilli sauce
1 spring onion (green onion), sliced

For the bang bang sauce
1 tsp soy sauce
1 tbsp reduced-sugar sweet chilli sauce
3 tbsp low-fat mayonnaise
1 tsp sriracha

In a bowl, mix together the sauce ingredients with 1 tablespoon of cold water. Stir well and set aside.

In a separate bowl, combine the chicken with the light soy sauce, garlic, and ginger, and stir to coat. Dust with the cornflour, then spray with oil and air-fry at 190°C (375°F) for 7 minutes. Turn and spray with oil once more, then cook for a further 5 minutes. Alternatively, cook the chicken in an oven preheated to 200°C (180°C fan/400°F/Gas 6) for 15 minutes or until cooked through. Set aside.

In a large bowl, mix the rice (no need to microwave it) with the grated carrot and peas. Add the dark soy sauce and sweet chilli sauce and stir well. Air-fry at 190°C (375°F) for 4 minutes, or tip into a frying pan and fry over a medium heat for 4–5 minutes.

Drizzle the bang bang sauce over the crispy chicken and toss to coat, then serve with the fried rice, with the sliced spring onion scattered over the top.

KCAL	CARBS	PROTEIN	FAT
447	66G	44G	4G

Taco-loaded potatoes

Prep 10 mins
Cook 20 mins
Serves 4
Freeze

As you're no doubt aware by now, I love crispy cubed potatoes or fries loaded with pretty much everything. Here, I've opted for all the classic taco flavours. It's delicious – and leftovers taste even better the next day.

800g (1¾lb) potatoes, diced into 2cm (¾in) cubes (I used Maris Piper)
2 tsp smoked paprika
1½ tsp garlic granules
1 tsp dried parsley
1 red onion, finely diced
1 red (bell) pepper, finely diced
3 garlic cloves, minced
500g (1lb 2oz) lean beef mince (ground beef)
25g (scant 1oz) taco seasoning
100g (3½oz) shop-bought salsa
1 beef stock cube
80g (2¾oz) reduced-fat Cheddar

For the sauce
5 tbsp light mayonnaise
3 tbsp low-fat sour cream
2 tsp taco seasoning
juice of ½ lime

In a bowl, toss the cubed potatoes with the smoked paprika, garlic granules, and dried parsley, mixing well to coat.

Air-fry at 200°C (390°F) for 15–20 minutes, shaking every 5 minutes. Don't overcrowd your air-fryer, or they will take longer to cook – use both drawers if you have them, or cook in batches. Alternatively, cook in an oven preheated to 220°C (200°C fan/425°F/Gas 7) for 20 minutes or until crispy, turning halfway through.

Meanwhile, spray a large frying pan with oil and fry the onion and pepper over a low–medium heat for a few minutes to soften. Add the minced garlic and beef, and fry for 3–4 minutes until browned, breaking up the meat with a spoon. Stir in the taco seasoning and salsa, then crumble in the beef stock cube, stirring it in with a dash of boiling water.

Combine the taco sauce ingredients in a bowl with 1 tablespoon water. Mix well and set aside.

When everything is ready, tip the crispy potatoes into a heatproof dish and top with the beef mixture, followed by the cheese. Grill (broil) on high for 1–2 minutes to melt the cheese. Finally, drizzle over your sauce and serve.

TIP Serve with lime wedges for squeezing to give it extra zing.

KCAL	CARBS	PROTEIN	FAT
473	48G	40G	13G

Garlic butter steak with cheesy mash

Prep 5 mins
Cook 15 mins
Serves 2
Freeze

This is one of my most popular recipes so far – and it's easy to see why. Cajun-seasoned steak bites served on top of cheesy, creamy mashed potatoes, with Cajun garlic butter to drizzle over the top … utter perfection.

250g (9oz) potatoes, peeled and diced
3½ tbsp semi-skimmed (2 per cent) milk
15g (½oz) low-fat butter
20g (¾oz) grated mozzarella
40g (1¼oz) low-fat Cheddar, grated
300g (10oz) lean rump steak (or any cut you fancy!), at room temperature
1 heaped tsp Cajun seasoning
spray oil
8 stalks Tenderstem broccoli (broccolini)
salt and freshly ground black pepper

For the Cajun garlic butter
10g (¼oz) low-fat butter
1 garlic clove, minced
pinch of Cajun seasoning
½ tsp dried parsley

Bring a large saucepan of salted water to the boil and add the potatoes. Cook for 15 minutes until fork tender, then drain and mash. Add the milk, butter, and both cheeses, and mix well until creamy. Add more milk to loosen if needed.

Season the steak with salt, pepper, and the Cajun seasoning, then spray with oil. Air-fry at 210°C (410°F) for 5–6 minutes (this will give you medium–rare steak), then leave to rest for a few minutes. Alternatively, spray a frying pan with oil and fry the steak over a medium–high heat for 3 minutes on each side.

Meanwhile, cook the broccoli in a small saucepan of boiling water for about 4 minutes or until tender, then drain.

To make the Cajun garlic butter, heat the butter, garlic and Cajun seasoning in a small bowl in the microwave for 10–15 seconds, or until the butter has melted, then stir in the dried parsley.

Divide the mash between 2 plates. Slice the steak into cubes and arrange on top, then drizzle over the garlic butter to finish. Serve with the broccoli. Enjoy!

KCAL	CARBS	PROTEIN	FAT
566	26G	49G	29G

Hot honey beef & sweet potato bowls

Prep 5 mins
Cook 15–20 mins
Serves 2
Freeze (sweet pot + beef)

This is inspired by a popular recipe I saw online, but I've given it my own spin. The combination of flavours – air-fried sweet potato, hot honey beef, and cottage cheese – sounds weird, but it works amazingly.

400g (14oz) sweet potato, diced into 2cm (¾in) cubes
spray oil
½ tsp ground cinnamon
250g (9oz) lean beef mince (ground beef)
1 tbsp taco seasoning
1 heaped tbsp tomato purée
1 beef stock cube
160g (5¾oz) cottage cheese
100g (3½oz) avocado, diced
salt and freshly ground black pepper

For the hot honey
1 tbsp honey
½ tsp chilli flakes
squeeze of lemon juice

Spray the sweet potato chunks with oil, then season with the cinnamon and some salt and pepper. Air-fry at 200°C (390°F) for 15–20 minutes, shaking every 5 minutes. If you have 2 drawers, use them both, as they'll cook quicker! Alternatively, cook in an oven preheated to 200°C (180°C fan/400°F/Gas 6) for 20–25 minutes, or until crispy and cooked through.

Spray a frying pan with oil and place over a medium heat. Fry the beef mince for a few minutes until browned, breaking it up with a spoon, then stir in the taco seasoning and tomato purée. Crumble in the beef stock cube and add a dash of boiling water, then stir to combine. Cook for a few minutes more.

To make the honey, combine the ingredients in a small saucepan and stir over a low–medium heat for a couple of minutes until runny. Alternatively, combine in a bowl and microwave for 10–15 seconds.

Divide the sweet potatoes and beef between two bowls, then pour the hot honey over the top. Serve with the cottage cheese and avocado.

TIP If you don't like cottage cheese, use Greek yogurt instead.

KCAL	CARBS	PROTEIN	FAT
546	57G	38G	20G

Cajun-style smash burger loaded fries

Prep 5 mins
Cook 18–20 mins
Serves 4
Freeze

A Cajun-seasoned smash burger loaded on to crispy fries, topped with cheese and drizzled with a super-addictive burger sauce? Hell yes.

500g (1lb 2oz) lean beef mince (ground beef)
1 heaped tbsp Cajun seasoning
spray oil
80g (2¾oz) low-fat Cheddar, grated
2 cheese singles, quartered
30g (1oz) onion, finely diced
4 gherkins (pickles), finely diced
salt and freshly ground black pepper

For the sauce
2 tbsp tomato ketchup
6 tbsp low-fat mayonnaise
1 tsp Worcestershire sauce
½ tsp garlic granules

For the homemade fries
800g (1¾lb) potatoes, cut into thin fries
2 tsp paprika
2 tsp garlic granules

TIP Don't overcrowd the air fryer when cooking the fries, and take care not to cut them too big, as they'll need longer to cook!

In a bowl, mix together the sauce ingredients with 2 tablespoons water, then set aside in the fridge.

To make the fries, season the potato strips with the paprika and garlic granules, along with a good pinch of salt. Air-fry at 200°C (390°F) for 15 minutes until golden, shaking often. Alternatively, cook in an oven preheated to 230°C (210°C fan/450°F/Gas 8) for 25–30 minutes.

Meanwhile, mix the beef mince with the Cajun seasoning, then roll into 8 equal-sized balls. Spray a large frying pan with oil, then place over a high heat. Add a few of the balls to the pan, then press down with spatula to form patties. Season well and fry for at least 3 minutes until the bottoms take on a lovely colour. Flip to cook on the other side, and cook for a couple of minutes more before breaking the patties into chunks using your spatula. Repeat with the rest.

Scatter the smash burgers over the cooked fries, then top with the grated Cheddar and cheese squares. Air-fry at 200°C (390°F) for 3–4 minutes until the cheese has melted, or return to the oven for 5 minutes.

Scatter the onion and gherkins over the top, then drizzle over the sauce and serve.

KCAL	CARBS	PROTEIN	FAT
451	43G	39G	13G

My ultimate red pesto tuna pasta bake

Prep 5 mins
Cook 20 mins
Serves 2
Freeze

Pasta bakes are super comforting, great for meal prep and real crowd-pleasers. Red pesto pairs so perfectly with tuna – and, of course, no pasta bake would be complete without plenty of cheese.

130g (4¾oz) fusilli pasta
spray oil
½ red onion, finely diced
½ red (bell) pepper, finely diced
80g (2¾oz) chestnut mushrooms, finely diced
2 garlic cloves, minced
30g (1oz) sun-dried tomatoes, diced
25g (scant 1oz) low-fat red pesto
2–3 basil leaves, finely sliced
1 chicken stock cube
250g (9oz) passata
2 × 160g (5¾oz) cans tuna in spring water, drained
20g (¾oz) Parmesan, grated
chopped flat-leaf parsley, to serve
salt and freshly ground black pepper

Cook the pasta according to the packet instructions until al dente, then drain, reserving a ladleful of the pasta water.

Spray a large frying pan with oil. Add the onion, pepper, and mushrooms, and fry over a medium–high heat for a few minutes to soften. Add the garlic, sun-dried tomatoes, pesto, and basil leaves, and fry for a minute more. Season with a good pinch of salt and pepper, then crumble in the chicken stock cube. Stir in the reserved pasta water and the passata, then add the tuna and cooked pasta and mix well to coat in the sauce.

Transfer to an ovenproof dish and top with the grated Parmesan. Air-fry at 180°C (350°F) for 8–10 minutes until the top is golden and bubbling. Alternatively, cook in an oven preheated to 200°C (180°C fan/400°F/Gas 6) for 13–15 minutes. Serve scattered with fresh parsley.

TIP Drizzle a little of the oil from the sun-dried tomato jar over the Parmesan before cooking for extra flavour.

KCAL	CARBS	PROTEIN	FAT
513	58G	53G	7G

Fajita beef-loaded crispy gnocchi

Prep 5 mins
Cook 15 mins
Serves 4
Freeze

Delicious fajita beef piled on to crispy air-fried gnocchi for amazing flavours and unbeatable crunch. It's great with guacamole and sour cream.

500g (1lb 2oz) gnocchi
spray oil
1 tsp paprika
1 tsp garlic granules
1 onion, finely diced
1 red (bell) pepper, finely diced
1 yellow (bell) pepper, finely diced
1 green (bell) pepper, finely diced
3 garlic cloves, minced
500g (1lb 2oz) lean beef mince (ground beef)
25g (scant 1oz) fajita seasoning
1 beef stock cube
1 heaped tbsp tomato purée
25g (scant 1oz) grated mozzarella
60g (2oz) low-fat Cheddar, grated
salt and freshly ground black pepper

For the chipotle sauce
100g (3½oz) fat-free Greek yogurt
1 tsp chipotle paste
juice of ½ lime
1 tsp honey

In a bowl, mix together the chipotle sauce ingredients with 2 tablespoons water, then set aside in the fridge.

Spray the gnocchi with plenty of oil, then season with the paprika, garlic granules, salt, and pepper. Air-fry at 200°C (390°F) for 13–15 minutes or until crispy, shaking every 5 minutes. Alternatively, tip into a lined baking tray and cook in an oven preheated to 200°C (180°C fan/400°F/Gas 6) for 20 minutes or until crispy.

Meanwhile, spray a lidded frying pan with oil and place over a medium heat. Fry the onion and peppers for a few minutes until softened, then add the garlic and fry for a further minute. Add the beef mince, breaking it up with a spoon, and fry for a few minutes to brown. Season with salt and pepper, then add the fajita seasoning and crumble over the stock cube. Mix well before adding the tomato purée and a dash of boiling water. Stir to combine, then scatter over both the cheeses. Cover with the lid and leave to steam for a couple of minutes until the cheese has melted.

Pile the fajita beef on top of the crispy gnocchi, and serve drizzled with the chipotle sauce.

KCAL	CARBS	PROTEIN	FAT
448	47G	40G	10G

Beef & spinach crispy tortellini

Prep 5 mins
Cook 15 mins
Serves 4
Freeze

I think this is the simplest recipe in the whole book. Seasoned beef mince is mixed with spinach and tortellini, and served with garlic bread. There – told you it was simple.

- 170g (5¾oz) shop-bought garlic bread
- 1 onion, finely diced
- 3 garlic cloves, minced
- 500g (1lb 2oz) lean beef mince (ground beef)
- spray oil
- 3 tsp Italian seasoning
- 2½ tsp paprika
- pinch of chilli flakes
- 435ml (scant 2 cups/14½fl oz) beef stock
- 300g (10oz) shop-bought filled tortellini (I used spinach and ricotta)
- 2 handfuls of spinach, roughly sliced
- 100g (3½oz) low-fat cream cheese
- 40g (1¼oz) Parmesan, grated
- salt and freshly ground black pepper

Cook the garlic bread according to the packet instructions.

Meanwhile, mix together the onion, garlic, and beef mince, then spray with oil. Air-fry without the crisper tray at 200°C (390°F) for 4 minutes. Use a spatula to break up the mince, then add the Italian seasoning, paprika, and chilli flakes. Season with salt and pepper and air-fry for a further minute before adding the beef stock and tortellini. Stir and air-fry for 4–5 minutes more, or until the tortellini is cooked, then stir in the spinach until wilted. Add the cream cheese, then air-fry for a further 1–2 minutes, or until the liquid is almost gone and it all looks wonderfully creamy.

Alternatively, spray a large saucepan with oil, then add the onions and fry over a medium heat for a few minutes to soften. Add the garlic and beef mince and fry for another 3–4 minutes, or until the beef has browned. Add the Italian seasoning, paprika, and chilli flakes, and season with salt and pepper. Scatter in the tortellini, then pour over the beef stock. Cover and cook for a further 6–8 minutes, or until the tortellini is al dente. Mix in the spinach until wilted, followed by the cream cheese.

Finish with the grated Parmesan and serve with the garlic bread.

KCAL	CARBS	PROTEIN	FAT
528	46G	43G	19G

Thai-style peanut & tofu noodles

Prep 5 mins
Cook 12-14 mins
Serves 2
Freeze

This veggie curry will keep you full and satisfied. The crispiest tofu pieces are mixed with a velvety, coconut-infused red Thai curry, topped with peanuts for a delicious crunch.

230g (8oz) firm tofu, drained, patted dry, and broken into chunks
spray oil
20g (¾oz) cornflour (cornstarch)
1 heaped tbsp red Thai curry paste
250ml (1 cup plus 1 tbsp/9fl oz) light coconut milk
½ red (bell) pepper, sliced
80g (2¾oz) sugar snap peas or mangetout (snow peas)
1 tsp crunchy peanut butter
1 tsp soy sauce
1 tsp honey
200g (7oz) straight-to-wok udon noodles
7g (¼oz) dry-roasted peanuts, lightly crushed
lime wedges, to serve

For the marinade
2 tsp soy sauce
2 tsp Thai red curry paste
2 tsp crunchy peanut butter

In a bowl, combine the marinade ingredients with a dash of boiling water and mix well. Add the tofu and stir to coat. Spray with oil and dust with the cornflour, then air-fry at 200°C (390°F) for 12–14 minutes until crispy. Alternatively, cook in an oven preheated to 220°C (200°C fan/425°F/Gas 7) for 20–25 minutes.

Meanwhile, spray a wok or large frying pan with oil and add the curry paste. Fry over a medium heat for a few minutes until fragrant, then pour in the coconut milk. Mix until well combined, then add the veggies. Fry for a few minutes to soften before stirring in the peanut butter, soy sauce, and honey. Add the udon noodles and fry for a further few minutes.

Divide the creamy noodles between 2 plates, then top with the crispy tofu. Sprinkle over the crushed peanuts and serve with lime wedges for squeezing.

KCAL	CARBS	PROTEIN	FAT
554	52G	25G	26G

WHY SPEND ALL THAT MONEY ON A TAKEAWAY WHEN YOU CAN MAKE A FAKEAWAY FOR A FRACTION OF THE PRICE? IT'S QUICKER THAN WAITING FOR A DELIVERY – AND THESE HOMEMADE VERSIONS ARE HEALTHIER, TOO.

BETTER THAN TAKEOUT

Panko peri peri halloumi ciabatta

Prep 5 mins
Cook 10 mins
Serves 2
Freeze (halloumi only)

I adore halloumi. I'm Mediterranean, so of course I've been eating this delicious cheese since I was a child, but as an adult I've experimented with it as an ingredient in dishes like this – and now, I love it even more.

- 200g (7oz) low-fat halloumi
- 1 tsp peri peri seasoning
- 1 tbsp plain (all-purpose) flour
- 1 egg, whisked
- 35g (1¼oz) panko breadcrumbs
- spray oil
- 2 tsp shop-bought peri peri sauce
- 3 tbsp low-fat mayonnaise
- 2 ciabatta rolls (about 60g/2oz each)
- handful of iceberg lettuce, sliced
- 1 tomato, sliced
- 1 heaped tbsp reduced-sugar sweet chilli sauce

Slice the halloumi block into 2 thick strips, then dust with the peri peri seasoning. Coat the first piece with plain flour, then dip into the whisked egg, followed by the panko breadcrumbs. Dip it into the egg once more, then the panko, so it's double-coated. Repeat for the second piece of halloumi.

Spray with oil and air-fry at 200°C (390°F) for 6–8 minutes until golden, flipping halfway and spraying with more oil. Alternatively, spray a frying pan with oil and place over a medium heat. Cook for 3–4 minutes before flipping and cooking for a further 2–3 minutes on the other side.

Mix the peri peri sauce with the mayonnaise and spread over the bottom halves of the ciabatta rolls. Top with the lettuce and tomato, followed by the crispy halloumi. Drizzle with the sweet chilli sauce, close the rolls and enjoy!

KCAL	CARBS	PROTEIN	FAT
538	51G	35G	21G

Crispy beef with vegetable fried rice

Prep 5 mins
Cook 20 mins
Serves 2
Freeze

Very similar to crispy chilli beef, but with a rich sauce that satisfies both sweet and savoury cravings. Make this next time you're tempted to get a takeaway.

1½ tsp soy sauce
2.5cm (1in) piece of fresh root ginger, minced
1 garlic clove, minced
400g (14oz) minute steaks
1 small egg, whisked
30g (1oz) cornflour (cornstarch)
spray oil
1 spring onion (green onion), sliced

For the fried rice
1 carrot, grated
100g (3½oz) frozen peas
250g (9oz) pouch microwaveable long-grain rice
1½ tbsp reduced-sugar sweet chilli sauce
2 tsp dark soy sauce

For the sauce
1 tbsp soy sauce
1 tbsp reduced-sugar sweet chilli sauce
squeeze of lemon juice
1 tsp honey
2.5cm (1in) piece of fresh root ginger, minced
1 garlic clove, minced
pinch of dried chilli flakes

In a bowl, combine the soy sauce, ginger, and garlic to make a marinade. Slice the steak into thin strips, then dip each strip into the marinade, then the whisked egg, and then the cornflour, turning to coat.

Spray the beef with oil and air-fry at 200°C (390°F) for 8 minutes, then turn and cook for a further 3–4 minutes until crispy. Use the crisper tray and work in batches if needed. Alternatively, arrange the beef on a lined baking tray and cook in an oven preheated to 220°C (200°C fan/425°F/Gas 7) for 18–20 minutes or until crispy, turning halfway through.

For the rice, combine the carrot, peas, and rice in a large bowl, then pour over the sweet chilli sauce and soy sauce. Mix well, then air-fry at 200°C (390°F) for 5 minutes, giving it a stir halfway through. Alternatively, cook the carrot and peas in a frying pan over a medium heat with a dash of boiling water for a few minutes. Once the water has evaporated, add the rice, sweet chilli sauce, and soy sauce. Increase the heat to high and fry for a few minutes more.

Combine the sauce ingredients in a frying pan over a high heat. Stir well and cook for 1–2 minutes until bubbling, then stir in the beef. Serve with the rice, topped with the sliced spring onion.

KCAL	CARBS	PROTEIN	FAT
567	70G	53G	9G

Thai red chicken curry

Prep 5 mins
Cook 15 mins
Serves 2
Freeze

A twist on a Thai red curry, this dish uses the sweetness of honey to bring all the flavours to life. The result is a super-bold curry that everyone will love. You can throw in any veggies you like if you want to bulk it out more.

- 100g (3½oz) basmati rice
- 250g (9oz) chicken breast, sliced
- 1 tsp paprika
- 2.5cm (1in) piece of fresh ginger, minced
- 2 garlic cloves, minced
- 50g (1¾oz) red Thai curry paste
- 200g (7oz) full-fat coconut milk (give it a good mix before using!)
- 80g (2¾oz) mangetout (snow peas)
- ½ red (bell) pepper, sliced
- 1 generous tsp soy sauce
- spray oil (optional)
- squeeze of lime juice
- 1 tsp honey
- salt and freshly ground black pepper

To serve

- freshly chopped coriander (cilantro)
- sliced red chilli (optional)

Cook the rice according to the packet instructions.

Meanwhile, season the chicken with salt, pepper, and the paprika.

In bowl, combine the ginger, garlic, curry paste, and a dash of the coconut milk, mixing well. Transfer to the air fryer without the crisper plate and air-fry at 190°C (375°F) for 2 minutes until fragrant. Add the mangetout and red pepper, then stir in the remaining coconut milk, along with the soy sauce and 3 tablespoons boiling water. Place the seasoned chicken on top of the veggies to stop them from burning, and air-fry at 200°C (390°F) for 10 minutes or until the chicken is cooked through, turning halfway.

Alternatively, spray a large frying pan with oil and place over a medium heat. Fry the ginger and garlic for a couple of minutes, then add the curry paste and cook for a few minutes more. Stir in the coconut milk, then add the veggies, seasoned chicken, and soy sauce. Simmer over a low–medium heat for 10–15 minutes or until the chicken is cooked through.

Finish with a good squeeze of lime and a drizzle of honey, then top with the coriander and some chilli slices, if using, and serve with the cooked rice.

KCAL	CARBS	PROTEIN	FAT
541	53G	36G	22G

Inside-out BBQ bacon cheeseburger

Prep 5 mins
Cook 7–8 mins
Serves 2

As soon as I came across inside-out burgers, I was dying to make my own. Now, I won't look back. Like a burger toastie, but better than you can imagine.

230g (8oz) lean beef mince (ground beef)
1 tsp garlic granules
1 tsp onion granules
spray oil
2 streaky bacon rashers (slices)
30g (1oz) low-fat Cheddar, sliced
2 brioche buns
4 tsp barbecue sauce
2 tbsp low-fat mayonnaise
salt and freshly ground black pepper

Season the beef with the garlic and onion granules, along with salt and pepper. Roll into 4 equal-sized balls, then flatten to form 4 burger patties.

Spray with oil, place on the crisper plate and air-fry at 200°C (390°F) for 4 minutes, along with the bacon. Remove from the air fryer and divide the cheese between 2 of the patties, then place the other patties on top. Place the bottom halves of the brioche buns in the air fryer, bottom-side up. Top with the double-stacked patties, followed by the barbecue sauce and bacon. Then turn the top halves of the buns upside down and place on top, gently pressing down, using toothpicks to hold everything together. Spray with oil and air-fry at 200°C (390°F) for 2–3 minutes until toasted.

Alternatively, spray a frying pan with oil and fry the patties over a high heat for 3 minutes or until the bottoms have caramelized, then flip and fry for a further 1–2 minutes. Add the cheese to 2 of the patties to melt. Remove them from the pan and set aside. Stack the buns, patties, sauce, and bacon as described above. Press down firmly and spray with oil, then fry for a few minutes on each side.

Once the burgers are ready, carefully open the lids and add the mayonnaise just before serving.

TIP These pair perfectly with my Homemade Fries (see page 109).

KCAL	CARBS	PROTEIN	FAT
384	29G	39G	12G

Sticky soy & garlic halloumi kebabs

Prep 5 mins
Cook 8-10 mins
Serves 2
Freeze

This lazy dinner is fast to prep and quick to cook. The halloumi and veggies are marinated in a soy sauce glaze and cooked on skewers, then served with a delicious sweet chilli mayo for dipping.

1 small onion, diced into bite-sized chunks
½ red (bell) pepper, diced into bite-sized chunks
80g (2¾oz) broccoli, broken into florets
180g (5¾oz) low-fat halloumi, diced into bite-sized chunks
1 tbsp soy sauce
1½ tsp dark soy sauce
1 tbsp honey
3 garlic cloves, minced
200g (7oz) microwaveable vegetable rice (or use precooked rice)

For the sweet chilli mayo
2 tbsp reduced-sugar sweet chilli sauce
3 tbsp low-fat mayonnaise

In a small bowl, combine the ingredients for the sweet chilli mayonnaise with 1 tablespoon cold water and set aside.

Grab a large bowl and add all the veggies and halloumi, then pour over both soy sauces, along with the honey and garlic. Mix well, then thread on to skewers and air-fry at 200°C (390°F) for 8–10 minutes, brushing any remaining marinade over the top during the last couple of minutes. Alternatively, grill (broil) on high for 8–12 minutes, brushing with the remaining marinade as above.

Meanwhile, prepare the rice according to the packet instructions.

Serve the kebabs with the rice, with the sweet chilli mayo drizzled over the top.

KCAL	CARBS	PROTEIN	FAT
523	61G	28G	61G

Chicken tikka in naan tacos

Prep 5 mins
Cook 10 mins
Serves 2
Freeze (chicken only)

I love a twist on a classic, and this is no exception. I used my two-ingredient dough to make the 'tacos', drizzled them with garlic butter and stuffed them with chicken tikka ... I still drool over these whenever I think about them.

85g (3oz) shop-bought skin-on fries
250g (9oz) chicken breast, butterflied
2 garlic cloves, minced
2.5cm (1in) piece of fresh ginger, minced
25g (scant 1oz) tikka paste
spray oil
1 tsp honey

For the naan tacos
100g (3½oz) thick fat-free Greek yogurt, plus extra to serve
100g (3½oz) self-raising flour, plus extra for dusting (or plain/all-purpose flour with 1½ tsp baking powder)
1 tbsp low-fat butter
1 garlic clove, minced
1 tsp freshly chopped coriander (cilantro)
pinch of salt

For the salad
2 tomatoes, deseeded and finely diced
50g (1¾oz) cucumber, diced
20g (¾oz) red onion, finely diced
squeeze of lemon juice

Cook the fries according to the packet instructions. In a bowl, mix together the salad ingredients and set aside.

Season the chicken with the ginger, garlic, and tikka paste, then thread on to skewers. Spray with oil and air-fry at 200°C (390°F) for 12 minutes, turning and spraying again halfway through. For the last minute, drizzle over the honey. Alternatively, grill (broil) on medium for 10–12 minutes, turning halfway through and drizzling over the honey for the last minute. Allow the chicken to rest before slicing.

Meanwhile, in a bowl, combine the yogurt, flour, and salt and mix to form a dough. Divide this into 4 equal-sized balls, then roll these out on a floured surface to create tacos. Spray a frying pan or griddle pan with oil and fry the naan tacos over a high heat for a couple of minutes on each side.

Heat the butter and garlic in a small bowl in the microwave for 10–15 seconds, or until the butter has melted, then stir in the coriander. Spread this over your naan tacos, then fill each one with a dollop of yogurt, the cooked chicken, the fries, and the salad. Enjoy.

KCAL	CARBS	PROTEIN	FAT
518	60G	40G	12G

Chinese-style chicken curry

Prep 5 mins
Cook 12 mins
Serves 2
Freeze

This kind of curry is a staple whenever we order a Chinese takeaway, so I was delighted to discover how easy it is to make at home. It's wonderfully creamy, and you get plenty of greens in by adding peas.

120g (4¼oz) basmati rice
220g (8oz) chicken breast, diced
4 tsp medium curry powder
½ onion, diced into large chunks
1 tbsp plain (all-purpose) flour
1 tsp cornflour (cornstarch)
100ml (3½fl oz) chicken stock
100ml (3½fl oz) semi-skimmed milk
150g (5½oz) frozen peas
spray oil
20g (¾oz) prawn crackers, to serve

Cook the rice according to the packet instructions.

Season the chicken with 1½ teaspoons of the curry powder.

Add the onion to the air fryer without the crisper plate, then arrange the chicken on top. Air-fry at 200°C (390°F) for 7 minutes. Add both flours and the remaining curry powder, then give it all a good mix before pouring in the stock, milk, and peas. Mix well again and air-fry for a further 8–10 minutes, or until the chicken is cooked through and the sauce has thickened.

Alternatively, spray a large frying pan with oil, then place over a high heat. Fry the onion for a few minutes to soften, then add the seasoned chicken and cook for 3 minutes until it has a nice colour. Reduce the heat to medium and continue to cook for a further few minutes. Next, add the plain flour and curry powder and mix well, then pour in the stock and milk. Cook for another couple of minutes before adding the peas. Simmer for 5–10 minutes more, or until the chicken is cooked and the sauce thickens. If you need to thicken it further, mix the cornflour with 2 teaspoons water to make a slurry, and stir this in.

Serve with the cooked basmati rice and prawn crackers.

KCAL	CARBS	PROTEIN	FAT
512	74G	40G	6G

Tandoori butter chicken

Prep 5 mins
Cook 12 mins
Serves 2
Freeze

250g (9oz) chicken breast, diced
spray oil
250g (9oz) pouch microwaveable rice
2 tsp low-fat butter
chopped coriander (cilantro), to serve

For the marinade
1 garlic clove, minced
2.5cm (1in) piece of fresh ginger, minced
2 tsp tandoori curry powder
1 tsp garam masala
45g (1½oz) fat-free Greek yogurt
squeeze of lemon juice
good pinch of salt

For the cheesy garlic naans
60g (2oz) self-raising flour, plus extra for dusting (or plain/all-purpose flour with 1 tsp baking powder and ¼ tsp salt)
70g (2¼oz) fat-free Greek yogurt
20g (¾oz) grated mozzarella
2 garlic cloves, minced
1 generous tsp low-fat butter
1 tsp fresh or dried parsley

For the sauce
1 garlic clove, minced
2.5cm (1in) piece of fresh ginger, minced
2 tsp tandoori curry powder
1 tsp garam masala
1 tsp ground coriander
200g (7oz) passata
1 chicken stock cube
45g (1½oz) fat-free Greek yogurt

If butter chicken and tandoori chicken had a baby, this would be it. Served with an easy, cheesy garlic naan to mop up the sauce.

Combine the marinade ingredients in a bowl. Add the chicken and stir to coat, then leave to marinate in the refrigerator, ideally for 30 minutes.

Spray the marinated chicken with oil and air-fry at 200°C (390°F) for 12 minutes until it takes on a lovely colour. For best results, use the crisper plate. Alternatively, arrange the chicken on a lined baking tray, preheat the grill to high, and grill for 13–15 minutes. Meanwhile, prepare the rice according to the packet instructions.

To make the naans, combine the flour and yogurt in a large bowl and mix to form a dough. Flatten it out slightly, scatter the cheese into the middle, then fold the dough over the top to conceal. Divide the dough into 2 equal-sized balls, then roll out on a floured surface to create 2 naans. Spray a frying pan with oil and fry the naans over a high heat for 2 minutes on each side. Meanwhile, heat the butter and garlic in a small bowl in the microwave for 10–15 seconds, or until the butter has melted, then stir in the parsley. Spread this mixture over each naan.

For the sauce, spray a frying pan or wok with oil and place over a medium heat. Add the garlic and ginger, along with all the spices, and fry for a few minutes. Add the passata, then crumble in the stock cube and add 2 tablespoons boiling water. Season with a good pinch of salt and mix well, then stir in the Greek yogurt, followed by the charred chicken pieces.

To finish, dot the butter over the top, then scatter with fresh coriander and serve with the cheesy naans and rice.

KCAL	CARBS	PROTEIN	FAT
548	61G	50G	12G

Satay king prawn pad Thai

Prep 5 mins
Cook 8–10 mins
Serves 2
Freeze

Whisk up this recipe for the quickest midweek dinner. It's packed with fragrant Thai flavours, chewy noodles, and delicious king prawns.

100g (3½oz) flat rice noodles
200g (7oz) raw king prawns (white shrimp), deveined and deshelled
1 tsp medium curry powder
1 tsp soy sauce
spray oil
½ red (bell) pepper, sliced
½ yellow (bell) pepper, sliced
2 garlic cloves, minced
2 eggs
juice of ½ lime
10g (¼oz) dry-roasted peanuts, lightly crushed
1 small red chilli, diced
1 spring onion (green onion), sliced

For the sauce
1 tbsp smooth peanut butter
2 tsp soy sauce
a few dashes of fish sauce
2 tsp soft light brown sugar or stevia
1 tsp white rice vinegar
juice of ½ lime

In a bowl, combine all the sauce ingredients with 1 tablespoon boiling water and mix well. Set aside.

Cook the noodles according to the packet instructions, then drain and set aside.

In a separate bowl, mix the prawns with the curry powder and soy sauce, then thread on to metal skewers. Spray with oil and air-fry at 200°C (390°F) for 4 minutes or until cooked through. Alternatively, grill (broil) the skewers on high for 2–3 minutes on each side. You can also use a griddle pan to cook them on the stove if you prefer.

Meanwhile, spray a large frying pan or wok with oil and place over a medium heat. Fry the peppers and garlic for a few minutes to soften, then move the peppers to one side of the pan, crack in the eggs and scramble until cooked to your liking. Stir in the drained noodles. Remove the prawns from their skewers and add to the pan, along with the sauce. Crank up the heat and stir well, making sure the sauce has coated everything evenly.

Serve with a squeeze of lime, topped with the chopped peanuts, red chilli, and spring onion.

KCAL	CARBS	PROTEIN	FAT
398	74G	40G	6G

Chilli chicken flatbreads

Prep 5 mins
Cook 15 mins
Serves 2
Freeze

All the flavours of crispy chilli beef, but with thin slices of crispy battered chicken. If you're a fan of the beef version, make sure you give this a shot.

250g (9oz) chicken breast, sliced into thin strips
2 garlic cloves, minced
2.5cm (1in) piece of fresh ginger, minced
2 tsp soy sauce
1 egg, whisked
25g (scant 1oz) cornflour (cornstarch)
½ onion, sliced
½ red (bell) pepper, sliced
½ yellow (bell) pepper, sliced
2 × 80g (2¾oz) flatbreads
1 spring onion (green onion), sliced

For the sauce
3 tbsp tomato ketchup
1 tbsp tomato purée
2 tsp soy sauce
1 tsp honey
squeeze of lemon juice
1 beef stock cube

In a bowl, combine all the sauce ingredients with a dash of boiling water and stir to combine. Set aside.

In a separate bowl, season the chicken strips with half the minced ginger and garlic, along with the soy sauce, then dip into the whisked egg and coat with the cornflour. Air-fry at 190°C (375°F) for 8 minutes, then crank up the heat to 200°C (390°F) and air-fry for an extra 5 minutes, or until lovely and crispy. Take care not to overcrowd the air fryer, working in batches if needed. Alternatively, cook the chicken strips in an oven preheated to 200°C (180°C fan/400°F/Gas 6) for 15–20 minutes.

Spray a large frying pan with oil and place over a medium heat. Add the onion, peppers, and remaining garlic and ginger, then cook for a few minutes to soften. Remove from the pan and set aside.

Return the empty pan to the heat and pour in the sauce. Crank up the heat to high and cook for a couple of minutes until bubbling. Add the crispy chicken and stir to coat, then return the veggies to the pan and mix it all together.

Lightly toast the flatbreads, then pile on the crispy chilli chicken. Scatter over the spring onion, then serve.

TIP The crispy chicken is also delicious served with rice or noodles.

KCAL	CARBS	PROTEIN	FAT
500	61G	45G	7G

Crispy salt & pepper beef

Prep 5 mins
Cook 12–14 mins
Serves 2
Freeze

A combo of my two favourite takeaway dishes: shredded crispy chilli beef and salt and pepper chicken. Serve with egg-fried rice and curry sauce, and I think you've just found your new favourite fakeaway.

400g (14oz) lean rump steak, at room temperature
4 tsp soy sauce
2 tsp five-spice powder
1 egg, whisked
25g (scant 1oz) cornflour (cornstarch)
spray oil
½ onion, finely diced
½ green (bell) pepper, finely diced
½ red (bell) pepper, finely diced
1 tsp granulated sugar or sweetener

For the egg-fried rice
60g (2oz) onion, finely diced
70g (2¼oz) frozen peas
1 egg, whisked
130g (4¾oz) cold cooked rice
1 tsp sesame oil
2 tsp dark soy sauce

To serve
1 spring onion (green onion), sliced
Chinese curry sauce (I use the Goldfish brand)

Tenderize the steak with a tenderizer or cover with cling film (plastic wrap) and bash with a rolling pin.

Slice it into thin strips, then season with half the soy sauce and half the five-spice powder. Dip each strip into the whisked egg, then coat with the cornflour. Spray with oil, then air-fry at 200°C (390°F) for 12–14 minutes. Alternatively, cook in an oven preheated to 220°C (200°C fan/425°F/Gas 7) for 15–20 minutes or until crispy.

Meanwhile, prepare the egg-fried rice. Spray a large frying pan with oil and place over a medium heat. Add the onion and peas and fry for a few minutes to soften, then add the egg and stir to scramble. Mix in the rice, followed by the sesame oil and dark soy sauce, and continue to cook until the rice is heated through.

Once the beef is ready, spray a second large frying pan or wok with oil and place over a medium heat. Fry the onion and peppers for a few minutes to soften, then stir in the remaining soy sauce and five-spice powder, along with the sugar. Add the crispy beef and stir everything to combine.

Serve the beef alongside the egg-fried rice, with a scattering of spring onion and some Chinese curry sauce for dipping or drizzling.

KCAL	CARBS	PROTEIN	FAT
380	20G	50G	11G

Cheese-crusted chicken burrito

Prep 5 mins
Cook 6–8 mins
Serves 1

Three words: crispy cheese crust. This burrito is coated on one side with this amazing cheesy crust, making it a super-fun recipe to make ... and eat.

spray oil
100g (3½oz) cooked chicken
1 tsp chipotle paste
1 tsp honey
squeeze of lime juice
100g (3½oz) microwaveable Mexican-style rice (or use precooked rice)
3 cherry tomatoes, finely diced
small handful of lettuce, sliced
1 tbsp finely diced red onion
2–3 jarred jalapeño slices
1 tortilla wrap
25g (scant 1oz) low-fat Cheddar, grated

For the chipotle sauce
2 tbsp plain yogurt
1 tsp chipotle paste
1 tsp honey
squeeze of lime juice

In a small bowl, combine all the chipotle sauce ingredients with 1 tablespoon cold water. Mix well and set aside.

Spray a frying pan with oil and place over a medium heat. Add the chicken, chipotle paste, honey, and lime juice, and fry for a few minutes to warm through. Meanwhile, cook the rice according to the packet instructions, and then heat the wrap in the microwave for 10 seconds.

Add the rice to the centre of the wrap, then top with the chicken, tomatoes, lettuce, onion, jalapeños, and half the chipotle sauce. Wrap up to create a burrito.

Turn on the air fryer at 200°C (390°F) for 5 minutes, leaving it empty. Once the air fryer is preheated, switch it off, then add the burrito, scattering the cheese over the top. Let it sit in the air fryer for a few minutes so the residual heat can slightly melt the cheese (otherwise it'll blow away!). Once it's slightly melted, air-fry at 200°C (390°F) for 3–4 minutes.

Alternatively, place a frying pan over a medium heat and scatter the grated Cheddar down the middle of the pan, giving it a few minutes to melt. Then add the burrito, seam-side down, pressing it on to the cheese. Cook for a couple of minutes to get the cheese to stick before frying on the other sides for a few minutes until golden.

Slice the burrito and serve with the remaining sauce for dipping or drizzling.

KCAL	CARBS	PROTEIN	FAT
514	62G	44G	9G

Loaded nachos with chipotle & lime chicken

Prep 5 mins
Cook 10–12 mins
Serves 2
Freeze (chicken only)

A super-fun dish loaded with cheese, shredded chicken, and all your favourite toppings. Perfect for a movie night. It always goes down so well!

300g (10oz) chicken breast, butterflied
1 tsp smoked paprika
1 tsp garlic granules
spray oil
60g (2oz) tortilla chips
40g (1¼oz) low-fat Cheddar, grated
salt and freshly ground black pepper

For the chipotle sauce
2 tsp chipotle paste
100g (3½oz) Greek yogurt
juice of ½ lime
1 heaped tbsp low-fat mayonnaise

For the salsa
10 cherry tomatoes, finely diced
40g (1¼oz) red onion, finely diced
1 coriander (cilantro) sprig, finely diced
juice of ½ lime
1 tsp olive oil

In a small bowl, combine the chipotle sauce ingredients with 1 tablespoon cold water and stir to combine. In a separate bowl, mix together the salsa ingredients and season with a pinch of salt. Set both aside.

Season the chicken with salt, pepper, and the smoked paprika and garlic granules. Spray with oil and air-fry at 200°C (390°F) for 12–14 minutes, flipping halfway and spraying with more oil. Alternatively, cook in an oven preheated to 200°C (180°C fan/400°F/Gas 6) for 20 minutes or until cooked through. Once the chicken is cooked, shred the meat using two forks.

Find a baking tray that fits your air fryer and line it with baking parchment. Add the nachos and scatter over the cheese. Air-fry at 200°C (390°F) for 3–4 minutes. Alternatively, melt under a hot grill (broiler). Top with the cooked chicken, then dollop over the sauce and salsa just before serving. Enjoy!

KCAL	CARBS	PROTEIN	FAT
483	28G	51G	18G

Chinese-style chicken with chips

Prep 5–10 mins
Cook 16 mins
Serves 2
Freeze

Crispy, tasty, satisfying ... to call this moreish would be an understatement. The secret to this recipe is a hint of sweetness in the salt and pepper mix.

150g (5½oz) shop-bought skin-on fries
360g (12¼oz) skinless, boneless chicken thighs, diced
2 tsp soy sauce
2.5cm (1in) piece of fresh root ginger, minced
1 garlic clove, minced
1 egg or egg white
25g (scant 1oz) cornflour (cornstarch)
spray oil
½ onion, diced
1 red (bell) pepper, diced
1 green (bell) pepper, diced
½ tsp five-spice powder
pinch of sweetener (or use sugar)
2 spring onions (green onions), sliced
handful of prawn crackers (shrimp crackers), to serve (optional)

For the glaze
2 tbsp reduced-sugar sweet chilli sauce
1 tsp dark soy sauce
1 tsp honey
squeeze of lemon juice

Cook the fries according to the packet instructions.

Meanwhile, add the chicken to a bowl with 1 teaspoon of the soy sauce, and the ginger and garlic. Toss to coat, then dip each chicken piece into the whisked egg or egg white, followed by the cornflour.

Spray the chicken with oil and air-fry at 190°C (375°F) for 7 minutes, then flip, spray again and cook for a further 7–9 minutes, or until the chicken is cooked through.

While the chicken is cooking, spray a frying pan with oil and place over a low–medium heat. Add the onion and peppers and cook for a few minutes to soften, then add your cooked chips, along with the five-spice and sweetener. Stir in the remaining 1 teaspoon of soy sauce and mix well, then divide the mixture between 2 plates.

Return the pan to the heat and add the glaze ingredients, along with 2 tablespoons water. Stir to combine, and cook on high until the mixture bubbles. Add the cooked chicken and stir to coat, then serve with the chips, topped with spring onions and with prawn crackers on the side!

KCAL	CARBS	PROTEIN	FAT
585	59G	40G	22G

Chicken Caprese stuffed-crust pizza

Prep 5-10 mins
Cook 12-14 mins
Serves 1
Freeze

Stuffed-crust pizzas blow my mind every time. Here, I've used my game-changing two-ingredient dough recipe to create a mozzarella-stuffed crust, topped with chicken, fresh basil, tomatoes, and a drizzle of balsamic glaze.

60g (2oz) self-raising flour, plus extra for dusting (or plain/all-purpose flour with 1 tsp baking powder)
70g (2¼oz) fat-free Greek yogurt
pinch of salt
50g (1¾oz) grated mozzarella
1 heaped tbsp tomato purée
pinch of dried oregano
75g (2½oz) cooked chicken, sliced
2 cherry tomatoes, quartered
2 tsp shop-bought low-fat pesto
a few basil leaves
drizzle of balsamic glaze (optional)

In a bowl, combine the flour and yogurt with a pinch of salt, and mix until a dough forms. Roll out on a floured surface to a thickness of 2–3mm (⅛in), then transfer to a lined baking tray.

Arrange 30g (1oz) of the grated mozzarella around the very edges of the pizza, then fold the dough over the cheese, pushing down gently to seal and create your stuffed crust. Spread the tomato purée over the middle of the base and sprinkle over the oregano. Top with the cooked chicken, tomatoes, and remaining mozzarella, then drizzle or dollop on the pesto.

Air-fry at 190°C (375°F) for 12–14 minutes until the cheese is melted and the dough is golden. Alternatively, cook in an oven preheated to 200°C (180°C fan/400°F/Gas 6) for 15–17 minutes.

Finish with the basil leaves and a drizzle of balsamic glaze, if you like, then serve.

KCAL	CARBS	PROTEIN	FAT
537	53G	47G	15G

Crispy perinaise chicken & chips flatbreads

Prep 5 mins
Cook 12–14 mins
Serves 2
Freeze (chicken)

This hits the spot every time. Crispy chicken and chips drizzled with a banging homemade perinaise, served atop a warmed flatbread.

60g (2oz) shop-bought skin-on fries
250g (9oz) chicken breast, cut into strips
2 tsp peri peri seasoning
4 tbsp shop-bought peri peri sauce
30g (1oz) cornflakes, crushed
1 egg, whisked
spray oil
2 × 80g (2¾oz) flatbreads
2 handfuls of iceberg lettuce
1 tomato, sliced

For the perinaise

1 tsp shop-bought peri peri sauce
2 tbsp low-fat mayonnaise

Cook the fries according to the packet instructions.

In a bowl, combine the perinaise ingredients with 1 tablespoon water, then set aside.

Season the chicken strips with 1½ teaspoons of the peri peri seasoning and 2 tablespoons of the peri peri sauce. In a shallow bowl, season the crushed cornflakes with the remaining ½ teaspoon peri peri seasoning.

Dip the chicken tenders into the whisked egg, then the cornflakes, turning to coat. Spray with oil and air-fry at 190°C (375°F) for 12–14 minutes or until cooked through, flipping halfway through. Alternatively, cook in an oven preheated to 200°C (180°C fan/400°F/Gas 6) for 15–20 minutes. Once the chicken is cooked, brush it with the remaining 2 tablespoons peri peri sauce.

Lightly toast the flatbreads, then fill with the chicken, lettuce, tomato slices, and cooked fries. Drizzle over the perinaise and enjoy.

TIP Try seasoning the fries with a pinch of peri peri seasoning for extra flavour.

KCAL	CARBS	PROTEIN	FAT
607	71G	44G	15G

IF YOU WANT TO IMPRESS YOUR LOVED ONE (OR EVEN TREAT A SPECIAL FRIEND), THESE DATE-NIGHT BANGERS WILL MAKE THEM EITHER MOVE IN OR MARRY YOU. THE CRÈME DE LA CRÈME OF RECIPES THAT YOU CAN'T WAIT TO SHARE WITH THE PEOPLE YOU LOVE THE MOST.

DATE-NIGHT BANGERS

Peri peri steak & garlic butter frites

Prep 5 mins
Cook 15 mins
Serves 2
Freeze

Cooking steak in the air fryer makes it extra juicy, while serving it with creamy peri peri sauce and garlic fries takes things to the next level. Use my Homemade Fries recipe on page 109 and you'll never look back.

400g (14oz) lean rump steak (or any lean steak), at room temperature
2½ tsp peri peri seasoning
spray oil
8 stalks Tenderstem broccoli (broccolini)
50ml (1¾fl oz) single (half and half) cream or alternative
1 heaped tsp shop-bought peri peri sauce
1 tsp red wine vinegar
½ beef stock cube
½ portion Homemade Fries (page 109)
a few slices of crusty white baguette, to serve (optional)

For the garlic butter
1 tbsp light butter
2 garlic cloves, minced
1 tsp fresh parsley, finely diced

Season the steaks with 2 teaspoons of the peri peri seasoning, then spray with oil and air-fry at 220°C (430°F) for 4 minutes, using the crisper plate. Flip and cook on the other side for a further 1–2 minutes. This will give you medium–rare steak. Alternatively, spray a frying pan with oil and fry the steaks over a medium–high heat for 2–3 minutes on each side. Set the meat aside to rest.

Cook the broccoli in a small saucepan of boiling water for about 4 minutes or until tender, then drain and set aside.

Meanwhile, in a saucepan over a medium heat, combine the cream with the peri peri sauce, red wine vinegar, and remaining peri peri seasoning. Crumble in the stock cube and stir. Cook for 1 minute or until the sauce thickens.

Meanwhile, heat the butter and garlic in a small bowl in the microwave for 10–15 seconds, or until the butter has melted, then stir in the dried parsley. Drizzle this mixture over the cooked fries and toss to coat.

Slice the steak, then serve it topped with the creamy sauce, with the fries on the side and some crusty bread for mopping up the sauce, if you like.

KCAL	CARBS	PROTEIN	FAT
530	39G	53G	18G

Triple-cheese lasagne

Prep 5 mins
Cook 20 mins
Serves 2
Freeze

This no-fuss lasagne saves you from heaps of washing-up, has all the cheesy goodness, and even incorporates a garlic breadcrumb topping. Stunning.

1 tsp paprika
1 tsp garlic granules
1 tsp dried parsley, plus a pinch to finish
200g (7oz) chicken breast, butterflied
spray oil
1 small onion, finely diced
½ red (bell) pepper, finely diced
350ml (1½ cups/12fl oz) chicken stock
70g (2¼oz) low-fat cream cheese
4 lasagne sheets, broken up
85g (3oz) shop-bought béchamel sauce
40g (1¼oz) grated mozzarella
1 tbsp grated Parmesan
salt and freshly ground black pepper
freshly chopped parsley, to serve

For the garlic breadcrumbs
20g (¾oz) panko breadcrumbs
1 tbsp low-fat butter
½ tsp garlic granules
½ tsp dried parsley

Combine the paprika, garlic granules, and dried parsley, and season with salt and pepper. Scatter half of this mixture over the chicken. Spray a frying pan with oil and fry the chicken over a medium heat for 3 minutes. Add the onion and red pepper, then flip the chicken and cook on the other side for a further 3 minutes.

Shred the chicken using two forks, then return it to the pan, along with the rest of the seasoning mixture. Add the stock and cream cheese and stir to combine, then submerge the lasagne sheets in the sauce. Cover and increase the heat to medium–high. Cook for 10 minutes until the pasta is al dente and most of the sauce has reduced.

Transfer the mixture into the air fryer, with the crisper plate removed. Dollop the béchamel over the top, then scatter over the cheeses, along with a pinch of dried parsley. Air-fry at 200°C (390°F) for 4–5 minutes until golden. Alternatively, transfer to an ovenproof dish, top with the béchamel and cheeses, and cook in an oven preheated to 200°C (180°C fan/400°F/Gas 6) for 15–20 minutes.

Toast the breadcrumbs in a pan over a medium heat for 3–4 minutes until golden. Add the butter, garlic granules, and parsley, and stir to melt the butter and combine.

Scatter the breadcrumbs over the top of the lasagne just before serving, along with the fresh parsley.

KCAL	CARBS	PROTEIN	FAT
526	48G	49G	16G

Firecracker pork stir-fry

Prep 5 mins
Cook 10 mins
Serves 4
Freeze

I created this recipe as a bit of an experiment, as I had some pork and wasn't sure what to do with it. I'm so happy with how it turned out! If you fancy an easy spicy stir-fry recipe, it doesn't get much better than this.

240g (8½oz) basmati rice
1 onion, finely diced
200g (7oz) broccoli, cut into small florets
spray oil
500g (1lb 2oz) lean pork mince (ground pork)
1 tbsp dark soy sauce
1 tsp red chilli flakes
1 red chilli, sliced
pinch of sesame seeds

For the sauce
2 tbsp light soy sauce
1 tbsp dark soy sauce
2 tsp honey
2 tbsp sriracha
4 tsp reduced-sugar sweet chilli sauce
2 tsp rice wine vinegar
1 chicken stock cube

TIP This recipe goes well with any stir-fry veg: think peppers, mange tout (snow peas), beansprouts – whatever you like.

Cook the basmati rice according to the packet instructions.

Meanwhile, in a bowl, combine the sauce ingredients, crumbling in the stock cube. Mix well and set aside.

Add the onion and broccoli florets to the air fryer without the crisper plate. Pour in a dash of boiling water and stir. Spray with oil and air-fry at 190°C (375°F) for 4 minutes, then remove the broccoli and set aside. Add the pork mince, soy sauce, and chilli flakes to the air fryer, breaking up the mince using a spatula. Air-fry at 200°C (390°F) for 5 minutes, then return the broccoli to the mixture and pour in the sauce, stirring well. Air-fry for a further 1–2 minutes until the pork is cooked through.

Alternatively, spray a large frying pan with oil and add the onion and broccoli. Fry over a medium heat for a few minutes to soften, then add a splash of boiling water and continue to cook for a further few minutes. Add the pork mince, soy sauce, and chilli flakes and fry for 5–6 minutes more until browned, then pour in the sauce, stirring to ensure everything is fully coated. Fry for a couple of minutes more, or until the sauce has thickened.

Serve the pork with the cooked basmati rice, topped with the sliced chilli and a scattering of sesame seeds.

KCAL	CARBS	PROTEIN	FAT
445	61G	35G	7G

Double smash chicken burger & peri peri fries

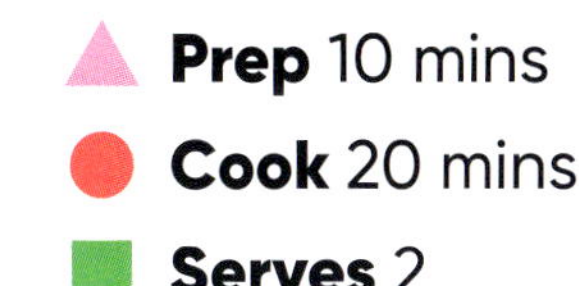

This is another of my most popular recipes. If you prefer, you can cook the burgers in the air fryer for super-juicy thick patties (see page 61 for timings).

250g (9oz) chicken mince (ground chicken)
2 tsp paprika
1 tsp garlic granules
50g (1¾oz) low-fat Cheddar, grated
2 brioche buns
handful of iceberg lettuce, sliced
1 tbsp finely diced onion
1 gherkin (pickle), sliced
salt and freshly ground black pepper

For the sauce
4 tbsp low-fat mayonnaise
2 tbsp tomato ketchup
½ tsp garlic granules
a few dashes of Worcestershire sauce

For the peri peri fries
400g (14oz) potatoes, cut into thin fries (I use Maris Piper)
spray oil
1 tsp paprika
1 tsp garlic granules
1 tsp peri peri seasoning (or peri peri salt!)

In a bowl, mix together all the sauce ingredients. Set aside.

Spray the fries with oil, and season with the paprika and garlic granules, along with a good pinch of salt. Air-fry at 200°C (390°F) for 15–20 minutes or until lovely and brown, shaking every 5 minutes. Alternatively, tip into a baking tray and bake in an oven preheated to 220°C (200°C fan/ 425°F/Gas 7) for 20–25 minutes or until crispy. Finish by sprinkling with the peri peri seasoning.

While the fries are cooking, season the chicken mince with the paprika and garlic granules, along with some salt and pepper. Divide into 4 equal-sized balls. Spray a large frying pan with oil and place over a high heat. Fry the patties for 2–3 minutes, pressing them down into the pan with a spatula. Flip, then fry on the other side for 2 minutes more. Top each patty with some cheese during the last minute and let it melt.

When everything is ready, lightly toast the brioche buns, then spread the bottom half of each bun with some of the sauce. Top with the lettuce, followed by the chicken patties and some more sauce, and then the onion and gherkin slices. Close the buns and serve with the peri peri fries.

KCAL	CARBS	PROTEIN	FAT
550	66G	44G	12G

Creamy coconut chicken curry

Prep 5 mins
Cook 15–16 mins
Serves 2
Freeze

The ultimate comfort meal: tender chicken simmered in a rich, flavourful coconut curry sauce that I could honestly drink. Simple yet satisfying.

300g (10oz) microwaveable sticky rice (or use precooked rice)
285g (9¾oz) chicken breast, diced
2 garlic cloves, minced
2.5cm (1in) piece of fresh ginger, minced
4 tsp oyster sauce
spray oil
1 tsp diced coriander (cilantro) stalks, plus leaves to serve
1 tsp curry powder
1 spring onion (green onion), sliced
25g (scant 1oz) red Thai curry paste
200g (7oz) full-fat coconut milk
1 tsp cornflour (cornstarch)
juice of 1 lime
4g (⅛oz) shop-bought crispy onions
salt and freshly ground black pepper

TIP Drizzle 1 teaspoon of chilli oil over the top as you serve for a spicy kick!

Prepare the rice according to the packet instructions.

In a bowl, combine the chicken with the garlic and ginger, along with half the oyster sauce. Season with salt and pepper and mix well, then thread on to skewers. Spray with oil and air-fry at 220°C (430°F) for 8 minutes until nearly cooked (if your air fryer doesn't go that high, just use the highest setting and cook for a few minutes longer). Alternatively, grill (broil) on high for 8–12 minutes, turning regularly.

Spray a frying pan with oil and place over a medium heat. Add the coriander stalks and curry powder, along with half the spring onion, and fry for a couple of minutes. Add the curry paste, along with the remaining oyster sauce, then spoon in a few teaspoons of the thick, creamy part of the coconut milk. Increase the heat to high for 1 minute, then add the remaining coconut milk and the cooked chicken. Reduce the heat to low–medium and simmer for a few minutes until the chicken is fully cooked through.

Combine the cornflour with 1½ teaspoons water to make a slurry, then stir this into the sauce to thicken. Lastly, squeeze over the lime juice.

Serve the curry with the sticky rice, topped with the remaining spring onion, crispy onions, and coriander leaves. Give it another squeeze of lime for a zesty hit!

KCAL	CARBS	PROTEIN	FAT
525	58G	40G	15G

Chicken pesto Milanese with spaghetti

Prep 5 mins
Cook 20 mins
Serves 2
Freeze

I added pesto to chicken Milanese and was amazed by how much it amplified the dish. Enjoy with a creamy tomato spaghetti and you can't go wrong.

120g (4¼oz) spaghetti
2 × 125g (4½oz) chicken breasts, butterflied
1 tsp Italian seasoning
1 tsp garlic granules
1 egg, whisked
30g (1oz) panko breadcrumbs
spray oil
2 tsp shop-bought low-fat pesto
10g (¼oz) grated mozzarella
10g (¼oz) Parmesan, grated
salt and freshly ground black pepper

For the sauce
1 tsp olive oil
3 garlic cloves, minced
10 cherry tomatoes, diced
4 basil leaves, sliced
pinch of chilli flakes
200g (7oz) canned chopped tomatoes
1 chicken stock cube
45ml (1½fl oz) single (half and half) cream

Cook the pasta according to the packet instructions, then drain and set aside, reserving a ladleful of the water.

Season the chicken with the Italian seasoning and garlic granules, along with some salt and pepper. Dip into the whisked egg, followed by the panko breadcrumbs, turning to coat. Spray with oil and air-fry at 190°C (375°F) for 8 minutes, then turn over, spray again, and cook for 5–7 minutes on the other side, or until cooked through. Alternatively, cook in an oven preheated to 200°C (180°C fan/400°F/Gas 6) for 20–25 minutes.

To make the sauce, heat the olive oil in a saucepan over a medium heat. Add the garlic and fry for a few minutes, then add the tomatoes, basil, and chilli flakes. Fry for 3 minutes, pressing down on the tomatoes with the back of a spoon. Add the chopped tomatoes and reserved pasta water, then crumble in the stock cube. Stir and simmer for a few minutes, then pour in the single cream. Take off the heat and blitz with a stick blender to form a creamy sauce.

Spread 1 teaspoon of pesto over each chicken breast, followed by 2 tablespoons of the sauce. Top with the mozzarella and air-fry for 3–4 minutes at 200°C (390°F). Alternatively, return to the oven and cook for 6–10 minutes. Mix the remaining sauce with the spaghetti and serve alongside the chicken, topped with grated Parmesan.

KCAL	CARBS	PROTEIN	FAT
555	62G	47G	14G

Sausage meatball carbonara

Prep 5-10 mins
Cook 10 mins
Serves 2
Freeze

A welcome spin on the classic carbonara, with crispy sausage meatballs to massively increase the protein content, keeping you fuller for longer.

120g (4¼oz) spaghetti
100g (3½oz) frozen peas
½ chicken stock cube
215g (7½oz) chicken sausages, skins removed
1 tsp Italian seasoning
1 garlic clove, minced
spray oil
2 slices shop-bought reduced-fat garlic bread
1 egg, plus 2 egg yolks
20g (¾oz) Parmesan, grated
salt and freshly ground black pepper
fresh flat-leaf parsley, to serve

Cook the pasta according to the packet instructions, adding the peas halfway through the cooking time. Drain and set aside, reserving a ladleful of the cooking water. Mix this with the stock cube and stir until fully dissolved.

Season the chicken sausage meat with the Italian seasoning, along with some salt and pepper. Add the garlic and mix well. Divide the mixture into 10–12 equal-sized meatballs. Spray with oil and air-fry at 200°C (390°F) for 8–10 minutes, shaking halfway through. Alternatively, spray a large frying pan with oil and fry over a medium heat for 10–12 minutes, turning often to brown all over.

Meanwhile, cook the garlic bread according to the packet instructions.

In a bowl, mix together the egg, egg yolks, Parmesan, and reserved pasta-water stock, and season with pepper.

If you're using the pan method, take the pan of meatballs off the heat. If you've been using the air-fryer method, place a large frying pan over a high heat to warm, then turn off the heat and add the meatballs. Add the cooked pasta and peas, along with the egg mixture. Stir until it turns creamy, then serve topped with the fresh parsley.

TIP You can use pork sausages or veggie ones instead of chicken, if you prefer.

KCAL	CARBS	PROTEIN	FAT
591	67G	42G	18G

Korean-style salmon bites & gochujang mayo

Prep 5 mins
Cook 7 mins
Serves 2
Freeze

If you like your food with a bit of a kick, then the Korean flavours in this dish will hit the spot. If you're not such a fan of the heat, you can always adjust the spice levels – but remember the gochujang mayo will cool things down!

2 skinless salmon fillets, each cut into 4 large chunks
2 tbsp low-fat mayonnaise
25g (scant 1oz) panko breadcrumbs
spray oil
250g (9oz) pouch microwaveable sticky rice (or use precooked rice)

For the sauce
1 tsp rice wine vinegar
½ tsp sesame oil
25g (scant 1oz) gochujang
2 tbsp tomato ketchup
1 tsp honey
1 tsp soy sauce
2 garlic cloves, minced
2.5cm (1in) piece of fresh ginger, minced

To serve
50g (1¾oz) cucumber, sliced
1 spring onion (green onion), sliced
sliced avocado (optional)
pickled sushi ginger (optional)

In a bowl, mix together all the sauce ingredients. Pour half the sauce over the salmon chunks, then mix the remaining sauce with the mayonnaise and 1 tablespoon cold water. Place this in the fridge.

Dip the sauce-coated salmon chunks into the panko breadcrumbs, then spray with oil and air-fry at 190°C (375°F) for 7–9 minutes. Alternatively, cook in an oven preheated to 180°C (160°C fan/350°F/Gas 4) for 10–15 minutes or until cooked through.

Meanwhile, prepare the rice according to the packet instructions.

Serve the salmon with the sticky rice and the rest of the sauce, along with the cucumber, spring onion, and optional avocado and pickled ginger.

KCAL	CARBS	PROTEIN	FAT
592	72G	30G	20G

Chilli prawn & chorizo linguine

Prep 5 mins
Cook 10 mins
Serves 2
Freeze

I don't know why prawns and chorizo go together so well, but they just do. The tomato pasta sauce offers a kick from the chilli flakes, while the parsley freshens it up wonderfully.

120g (4¼oz) linguine
40g (1¼oz) chorizo, diced
200g (7oz) raw king prawns, deveined and deshelled
60g (2oz) shallots or onion, finely diced
2 garlic cloves, minced
12 cherry tomatoes, halved
1 heaped tbsp tomato purée
100ml (3½fl oz) vegetable stock
4–5 basil leaves, sliced
salt and freshly ground black pepper
grated Parmesan, to serve (optional)

Cook the linguine according to the packet instructions, then drain and set aside, reserving a ladleful of the cooking water.

Meanwhile, air-fry the chorizo and prawns at 200°C (390°F) for 5 minutes without the crisper plate, stirring halfway through. Remove the prawns and chorizo and set aside, then add the shallots or onion to the air fryer, along with the garlic, cherry tomatoes, tomato purée, and stock. Season and mix well, then air-fry at 200°C (390°F) for 6 minutes. Gently crush the cherry tomatoes, then stir in half the basil, along with the prawns, linguine, and reserved pasta water.

Alternatively, fry the chorizo in a frying pan over a medium heat for 3 minutes, then set aside. In the same pan, fry the shallots or onion for a few minutes until softened, then add the garlic, cherry tomatoes, and tomato purée, along with half the basil. Season, then stir in the reserved pasta water and cook for 2 minutes more before adding the stock and prawns. Simmer for 3–4 minutes until the prawns are cooked through, using the back of the spoon to crush the tomatoes and create a sauce. Stir in the cooked linguine.

To serve, top the pasta with the rest of the basil and the crispy chorizo, along with a grating of Parmesan, if you like.

TIP If you prefer, you can use parsley instead of basil.

KCAL	CARBS	PROTEIN	FAT
491	48G	37G	16G

Crispy peppercorn chicken baguette

Prep 5 mins
Cook 12–14 mins
Serves 2

A delectable peppercorn sauce drizzled over crispy cornflake-coated chicken in a crusty baguette. This makes a truly banging dinner that your lucky date-night partner will be asking for again and again.

150g (5½oz) bake-at-home baguette
250g (9oz) chicken breast, sliced into strips
1 tsp chicken seasoning
1 egg, whisked
40g (1¼oz) cornflakes, crushed
50g (1¾oz) light mozzarella, diced
60g (2oz) low-fat coleslaw
2 handfuls of mixed leaves (or salad of your choosing)
salt and freshly ground black pepper

For the sauce
spray oil
2 tsp freshly ground black pepper
1 small onion, finely diced
50ml (1¾fl oz) chicken stock
50g (1¾oz) low-fat crème fraîche
1 tsp chicken seasoning

Cook the bake-at-home baguette according to the packet instructions.

Season the chicken strips with salt, pepper, and the chicken seasoning. Dip the seasoned strips into the whisked egg, then the cornflakes, turning to coat. Air-fry at 190°C (375°F) for 12–14 minutes, flipping halfway.

Meanwhile, make the sauce. Spray a saucepan with oil and place over a low–medium heat. Add the black pepper and onion, and fry for a few minutes until softened. Add the chicken stock, along with the crème fraîche, and mix well, then season with the chicken seasoning and a little more black pepper to taste. When the sauce starts to thicken, it's ready to go.

Slice the baked baguette in half, then slice open each half and add the chicken strips. Top with the mozzarella, then pour over the pepper sauce. Serve with the mixed leaves and coleslaw.

KCAL	CARBS	PROTEIN	FAT
600	67G	48G	11G

Steak stroganoff tagliatelle

Prep 5 mins
Cook 10 mins
Serves 2
Freeze

Instead of slicing the steak and cooking it in the sauce, this recipe calls for the steak to be cooked first, then served on top of pasta. It's a tasty variation that takes things to the next level.

120g (4¼oz) tagliatelle
400g (14oz) lean rump steak (or any lean cut), at room temperature
2 tsp paprika
1 tsp garlic granules
1 tsp dried parsley
spray oil
2 streaky bacon rashers (slices)
8 chestnut mushrooms, sliced
1 tsp Dijon mustard
45g (1½oz) low-fat crème fraîche
a few dashes of Worcestershire sauce
1 beef stock cube
freshly chopped parsley, to serve

Cook the pasta according to the packet instructions, then drain, reserving a ladleful of the cooking water.

Meanwhile, season the steak with salt and pepper, along with 1½ teaspoons of the paprika, and the garlic granules and dried parsley. Spray with oil and rub in the seasonings.

Air-fry the steak and bacon at 220°C (430°F) for 4 minutes. Flip the steak, then cook for a further 1–2 minutes on the other side. This will give you medium-rare steak. For best results, use the crisper tray, and work in batches or use the second drawer if you have one. Alternatively, spray a frying pan with oil and fry the steak and bacon over a medium heat for 2–3 minutes on each side. Set aside to rest.

Spray a frying pan with oil and place over a medium heat (if you used the pan method above, you can use the same frying pan here). Fry the mushrooms for a few minutes to soften (see tip), then stir in the remaining paprika, along with the mustard, crème fraîche, and Worcestershire sauce. Crumble in the stock cube, and stir in the reserved pasta water. Cook for 1–2 minutes or until the sauce thickens.

Divide the pasta between 2 bowls and top with the mushrooms. Slice the steak and arrange it on top of the pasta, then chop the bacon and scatter it over the top. Finish with some parsley to serve.

TIP If the steak releases any juices in the air fryer, stir these into the mushroom mixture.

KCAL	CARBS	PROTEIN	FAT
563	48G	57G	17G

Peri peri chicken filo bake

Prep 5 mins
Cook 20 mins
Serves 2
Freeze (filling)

This is a real statement pie. It's filled with creamy peri peri chicken and topped with filo pastry that goes super crispy in the air fryer for a texture sensation.

- 225g (8oz) chicken breast, diced into small chunks
- 2 tsp peri peri seasoning
- 1 tbsp + 1 tsp peri peri sauce
- spray oil
- ½ onion, finely diced
- ½ red (bell) pepper, finely diced
- 100ml (3½fl oz) chicken stock
- 55g (2oz) low-fat cream cheese
- 1 tsp cornflour (cornstarch)
- 60g (2oz) shop-bought filo pastry

Season the chicken with 1 teaspoon of the peri peri seasoning and 1 tablespoon of the peri peri sauce.

Spray a frying pan with oil and place over a medium–high heat. Fry the onion and red pepper for a few minutes to soften, then move the veggies to the side of the pan and add the chicken. Cook for a few minutes, or until the chicken has a nice colour at the bottom, then flip and cook on the other side for a few minutes more. Add the stock, cream cheese, and remaining peri peri seasoning and peri peri sauce. Mix the cornflour with 1½ teaspoons water to make a slurry, then stir this in to help thicken the sauce.

Transfer the mixture to an ovenproof dish, then scrunch the filo pastry on the top and spray with oil. Air-fry at 180°C (350°F) for 8–10 minutes until the pastry is golden and crispy. Alternatively, bake in an oven preheated to 200°C (180°C fan/400°F/Gas 6) for 13–15 minutes.

Serve and enjoy.

TIP This is delicious served with cheesy mashed potatoes and broccoli.

KCAL	CARBS	PROTEIN	FAT
306	30G	34G	6G

Sticky beef bulgogi bowls

Prep 10 mins
Cook 8 mins
Serves 2
Freeze (except cucumber)

The perfect balance of sweet, savoury, and umami – ideal for a quick, no-fuss meal that still feels special enough for date night.

120g (4¼oz) short-grain rice
½ onion, finely diced
250g (9oz) lean beef mince (ground beef)
2 spring onions (scallions), cut into matchsticks
spray oil (optional)

For the sauce
2 garlic cloves, minced
1 tbsp gochujang
1 tsp sesame oil
2 tbsp soy sauce
2 tsp honey

For the pickled cucumber
80g (2¾oz) cucumber, thinly sliced
1 tbsp rice wine vinegar
½ tsp granulated sugar

To serve
2 fried eggs
sesame seeds, for sprinkling
kimchi (optional)

Cook the rice according to the packet instructions.

In a small bowl, combine the sauce ingredients with 1–2 tablespoons boiling water. Mix and set aside.

In a separate bowl, combine the pickled cucumber ingredients and leave to marinate for at least 10 minutes, then drain.

Add the onion to the air fryer without the crisper plate. Pour in a dash of boiling water and air-fry at 200°C (390°F) for 3 minutes, then add the mince and spring onions, using a spatula to break the beef apart. Air-fry at the same temperature for 3–4 minutes until browned, then pour in the sauce, mix well and air-fry at 220°C (430°F) for another 2 minutes.

Alternatively, spray a frying pan with oil and fry the onion over a medium heat for 3–4 minutes to soften. Add the beef mince and fry for 3–4 minutes until browned, then mix in the spring onions. Pour in the sauce and increase the heat to high. Cook for a couple of minutes more, stirring until everything is coated and the sauce has thickened.

Pile the beef on top of the rice, then serve topped with the pickled cucumbers, along with the fried eggs, sesame seeds, and kimchi, if using.

TIP For a kick of heat, add 1 teaspoon chilli oil to the pickled cucumber marinade.

KCAL	CARBS	PROTEIN	FAT
539	62G	40G	14G

Pancetta chicken Alfredo

Prep 5 mins
Cook 10–12 mins
Serves 2
Freeze

A winning pasta recipe sure to impress. This comes approved by my husband, who doesn't normally like creamy dishes! (I know, he's an odd one.)

100g (3½oz) tagliatelle
70g (2¼oz) shop-bought garlic bread
225g (8oz) chicken breast, diced
1 tsp paprika
½ tsp garlic granules
½ tsp mixed herbs
40g (1¼oz) smoked pancetta
1 small onion, finely diced
25g (scant 1oz) garlic-and-herb soft cheese (I like Boursin)
2 tbsp single (half and half) cream
squeeze of lemon juice
1 tbsp grated Parmesan
8 stalks Tenderstem broccoli (Broccolini)
salt and freshly ground black pepper

Cook the pasta according to the packet instructions, then drain, reserving a couple of tablespoons of the water. Cook the garlic bread according to the packet instructions.

Meanwhile, season the chicken with salt and pepper, along with the paprika, garlic granules, and mixed herbs.

Remove the crisper plate from the air fryer and air-fry the pancetta at 200°C (390°F) for 4–6 minutes until crisp, then remove and set aside. Air-fry the chicken for 5 minutes, then add the onion and air-fry for a few minutes more. Stir in the cream cheese, cream, and reserved pasta water, along with half the Parmesan. Add the lemon juice and pasta, and air-fry for 3–5 minutes until the sauce thickens.

Alternatively, fry the pancetta in a frying pan over a medium–high heat for 4–6 minutes until crisp, then set aside. In the same pan, fry the onion for 2–3 minutes, then add the chicken. Fry for 5–6 minutes, then stir in the cream cheese, cream, pasta water, lemon juice, and half the Parmesan. Cook for a few minutes more until the sauce thickens, then stir in the tagliatelle.

Meanwhile, cook the broccoli in a small saucepan of boiling water for about 4 minutes or until tender, then drain.

Serve the pasta topped with the pancetta and remaining Parmesan, with the garlic bread and broccoli on the side.

KCAL	CARBS	PROTEIN	FAT
599	53G	47G	19G

Red pesto veggie sausage traybake

Prep 5 mins
Cook 20 mins
Serves 2
Freeze

I love a traybake, as they are super simple. Just bang it all in one dish and you're ready to roll.

- 400g (14oz) potatoes, diced into 2cm (¾in) cubes
- 1 small courgette (zucchini), chopped into bite-sized pieces
- ½ red onion, chopped into bite-sized pieces
- 8 cherry tomatoes
- ½ orange or yellow (bell) pepper, chopped into bite-sized pieces
- 2 tbsp shop-bought low-fat red pesto
- 6 veggie sausages (I love Richmond Meat-free Sausages!)
- 80g (2¾oz) low-fat mozzarella
- basil leaves, to serve

Add the potatoes, courgette, onion, tomatoes, and pepper to the air fryer without the crisper plate. If you have two drawers, use both; if not, it may take a little longer for everything to cook.

Add half the pesto and stir to coat, then place the sausages on top. Air-fry at 200°C (390°F) for 10 minutes, then remove the sausages and give the veggies a really good mix. Place the sausages back on top and air-fry for a further 7 minutes. Remove the sausages again and set aside to keep warm. Stir the veggies once more, then add the mozzarella and remaining pesto. Crank up the heat to 220°C (430°F) and air-fry for a further 3 minutes or until the cheese is melted and the vegetables are cooked through.

Alternatively, tip the veggies into an ovenproof dish and top with the sausages. Cook in an oven preheated to 200°C (180°C fan/400°F/Gas 6) for 30 minutes, then remove the sausages and give the veggies a mix. Place the sausages back on top and cook for 10 minutes more. Stir in the mozzarella and pesto, then cook for a final 5 minutes.

Divide between 2 plates, scatter over the fresh basil and dive right in!

KCAL	CARBS	PROTEIN	FAT
477	57G	25G	15G

Cajun-style prawn spaghetti

Prep 5 mins
Cook 10 mins
Serves 2
Freeze

I love the Cajun flavours in this dish, and when it's paired with a cheesy garlic bread, you really can't go wrong.

120g (4¼oz) spaghetti
200g (7oz) raw king prawns (white shrimp), deveined and deshelled
spray oil
1 tbsp Cajun seasoning
½ onion, finely diced
2 garlic cloves, minced
1 heaped tbsp tomato purée
100ml (3½fl oz) chicken stock
50g (1¾oz) low-fat cream cheese
salt

For the garlic bread
2 tsp low-fat butter
1 garlic clove, minced
pinch of dried parsley
70g (2¼oz) flatbread
30g (1oz) grated mozzarella

To serve
squeeze of lemon juice
15g (½oz) Parmesan, grated
freshly chopped parsley

Cook the spaghetti according to the packet instructions, then drain, reserving a ladleful of the cooking water.

Spray the prawns with oil and season with half the Cajun seasoning. Thread on to skewers and spray with oil again, then air-fry at 200°C (390°F) for 4 minutes. Alternatively, grill (broil) on high for 2–3 minutes on each side until nicely coloured and cooked through.

Meanwhile, spray a frying pan with oil and fry the onion over a medium heat for a few minutes to soften. Add the garlic and cook for a minute more, then add the tomato purée and the remaining Cajun seasoning. Fry for a further minute, then add the chicken stock, cream cheese, and reserved pasta water. Simmer for a few minutes until wonderfully creamy, then stir in the spaghetti.

Meanwhile, make the garlic bread. Combine the butter, garlic, and parsley, then spread over the flatbread. Top with the mozzarella, pressing it down so it sticks to the butter. Air-fry at 190°C (375°F) for 4–5 minutes until the cheese has melted. Alternatively, cook in an oven preheated to 200°C (180°C fan/400°F/Gas 6) for 10 minutes.

To serve, divide the spaghetti between 2 plates or bowls, then top with the cooked prawns. Finish with a good squeeze of lemon and a scattering of Parmesan and parsley, and serve with the garlic bread.

KCAL	CARBS	PROTEIN	FAT
549	68G	40G	14G

Acknowledgments

I want to thank my literary agent Amanda for making this book possible, for always believing in my visions and for giving me all the support I need. To the team at DK Red, thank you for all your work in bringing this amazing book to life. To the incredibly talented food photographer Ellis, whom I just couldn't do a book without, you smash it every time. To my husband, mum, and grandparents, who are always cheering me on through every life adventure, even when things get tough. Thank you for always having my back. To my daughter Sophia, my beautiful, chaotic whirlwind, you have brought so much love into our lives and you give me so much strength. I hope I have made you proud. A massive thank you also to my online community. Without you, none of these books would have been possible.

Lastly, I want to dedicate this book to my cousin whom I call my sister, Jasmine. You are fighting each day to heal after three major surgeries to remove your brain tumour. I love you an unbelievable amount and pray each day for you to get better, so you can hold your goddaughter Sophia in your arms again.

You're the strongest and bravest woman I know.

About the author

Christina Kynigos (@veryhungrygreek) is a *Sunday Times* bestselling author, "air fryer queen" and a high-energy TikTok sensation who, since starting her account in 2020, has amassed over 1.5 million followers across social media platforms with her low-calorie, high-protein recipes. Christina writes delicious recipes that make eating healthily very easy indeed, and her cookbooks include recipes that will feed – and please – everyone.

Christina has authored two *Very Hungry Greek* cookbooks featuring slimming recipes that push the boundaries on what's achievable in low-calorie cooking. Her last cookbook, *Healthy Air Fryer Feasts*, was published in 2024 and was an instant *Sunday Times* bestseller.

Index

Note: page numbers in **bold** refer to recipe illustrations.

D

E

F

P

R

S

T

V

DK LONDON
Editorial Director Cara Armstrong
Project Editor Izzy Holton
Food & Drink Design Manager Tania Gomes
Senior Production Editor Tony Phipps
Senior Production Controller Stephanie McConnell
Art Director Max Pedliham
Publishing Director Stephanie Jackson

Editorial Tara O'Sullivan
Design Hello Daly
Photography Ellis Parrinder
Food Styling Sonali Shah
Prop Styling Daisy Shayler-Webb
Food Styling Assistant Kristine Jakobsson

First American Edition, 2025
Published in the United States by DK Publishing,
a division of Penguin Random House LLC
1745 Broadway, 20th Floor, New York, NY 10019

Text copyright © 2025 Christina Kynigos
Christina Kynigos has asserted her right
to be identified as the author of this work.

Copyright © 2025 Dorling Kindersley Limited
25 26 27 28 29 10 9 8 7 6 5 4 3 2 1
001–356865–Nov/2025

All rights reserved.
Without limiting the rights under the copyright reserved above, no part of this publication may be reproduced, stored in or introduced into a retrieval system, or transmitted, in any form, or by any means (electronic, mechanical, photocopying, recording, or otherwise), without the prior written permission of the copyright owner.
No part of this publication may be used or reproduced in any manner for the purpose of training artificial intelligence technologies or systems. In accordance with Article 4(3) of the DSM Directive 2019/790, DK expressly reserves this work from the text and data mining exception.
Published in Great Britain by Dorling Kindersley Limited.

ISBN: 979-8-2171-3815-9

Printed and bound in Germany

www.dk.com

This book was made with Forest Stewardship Council™ certified paper – one small step in DK's commitment to a sustainable future.
Learn more at www.dk.com/uk/information/sustainability